MW00848633

TURN OF THE WORLD

By
ELIZABETH, LADY DECIES

TURN OF THE WORLD
"KING LEHR"
AND THE GILDED AGE

Wide World photo.

LORD AND LADY DECIES AFTER THEIR CIVIL MARRIAGE
MAY 25, 1936

ELIZABETH, LADY DECIES
ELIZABETH WHARTON DREXEL

TURN OF THE WORLD

WITH 34 ILLUSTRATIONS

PUBLISHED IN COOPERATION WITH
THE PRESERVATION SOCIETY OF NEWPORT COUNTY

APPLEWOOD BOOKS
CARLISLE, MASSACHUSETTS

Turn of the World by Lady Decies
was originally published by J.B. Lippincott Company in 1937.

Cover photograph by Dupont, New York
appeared in *Munsey's Magazine*, 1899.

ISBN: 978-1-4290-9080-3

Thank you for purchasing an Applewood book.
Applewood reprints America's lively classics—
books from the past that are still of
interest to modern readers.
Our mission is to build a picture of the past
through primary sources.

To request a free copy
of our current print catalog
featuring our best-selling books, write to:
Applewood Books
P.O. Box 27
Carlisle, MA 01741
For more complete listings,
visit us on the web at:
www.awb.com

Manufactured in the United States of America

CONTENTS

ILLUSTRATIONS

CHAPTER I

THE CELLAR

AS I THINK OF IT NOW WE WERE CROUCHING, YET, UNLIKE many who were that night hiding for the first time underground, we had light and warmth; we were huddled around the furnace. We were holding our breath. There were eight of us, including the two Swiss chauffeurs who were the only men-servants we had after the footmen had gone to the war and the butler had been arrested because he was a German. The cook and the housemaids were praying, the hands in which they held their rosaries were shaking. Whenever a crash was heard, the praying stopped.

"Where did that fall?"

No one knew, and the prayers began again.

There was a servants' dining-room in the basement where we would have been more comfortable, but the Government Engineer who had inspected our refuge from German bombs had told us that it was not safe: "There are not enough floors between you and the roof," he had said. The dining-room was under our hall, which was two stories high. Everyone had admired its lofty spaciousness. Now we wished that it had been like other halls. The more floors above you when you had to hide in the cellar the safer you were!

The kitchen would have been better too but it had windows on the street-side and we should have had to sit in complete darkness. Here in the furnace-room there were no windows, and there were as many floors above us as the house possessed. Comforting too, was the fact that it was vaulted.

Wicked-looking hooks had attracted my attention when the Government Engineer was inspecting this room and I had asked what they were for.

"For game," he said. "This room served as a refrigerator in the days when they had no other kind."

So, as we sat half-crouching on the chairs which we had brought from the dining-room, I imagined venison and wild boar hanging here while banquets were being prepared in the kitchen and the hosts were upstairs in those gorgeous costumes, which harmonized so much better than ours of today with the panelled walls and rich decoration of the period. All that, I could see in a flash while we were bent over as though we had little confidence that the vaulted ceiling would protect us.

From the furnace-room there was a door opening on the opposite side into the dark from which came the smell of damp and a cold current of air. We had opened it because the Engineer had told us to. He said it must be left open. It led to the cellar of our proprietor, the Marquis de Nicolay, whose house we shared. He had an outside door to his basement and so had we; if one were cut off by falling walls, the other might still be used. The pickaxe and shovel leaning up against the furnace looked sinister but they might save our lives in case both ways to the open were denied us.

From that dark room came voices. We recognized them as belonging to the Marquis and to his brother, Count Antoine. They had no light in the room where they were; their kitchen, like ours, had windows on the street and could not now be used. And we knew that there was no furnace. There had been none at all in the house until we had installed it. We went to the door and asked the two men, whom we could hear but could not see, to come in.

The Marquis de Nicolay appeared on the threshold, an aristocratic man of seventy, rather sketchily dressed and wearing a huge muffler; following him was his brother who was much younger. The servants stayed behind. They were safe even if they were not comfortable.

"We *may* be killed by a bomb," said the Marquis, "but I shall most certainly die of rheumatism if we stay in that cold, damp cellar."

Two more chairs were brought and we made a place close to the furnace for them. We did not talk. We were listening. But now whenever a distant crash was heard and the prayers stopped ior a moment, the Marquis would say, "That fell near the Opera" or "Somewhere along the Boulevard de Saint-Germain."

Up there in the air an eye was still peering down

upon Paris and a mind deciding where to let the next bomb fall!

And Paris was hiding underground with as many floors above it as it could muster!

As a social affair this first evening underground was unique. Here we were, Americans, entertaining two well-known members of the French noblesse, but our feeble attempt at conversation was interrupted by many pauses while we strained our ears for sounds from the outer world. We were here because we had come back to do what little we could in the American Ambulance service; the Marquis and his brother were here only because they were too old to go to war.

The Marquis, who had never married—it was said because he preferred his racing stable to the doubtful joys of domesticity—had the companionship of his devoted brother, Count Antoine, a widower whose two sons were at the front.

"What would my father say if he could see us here?" said the Marquis, with a look towards that dark room from which he had just emerged. He had, he told us, experienced the Franco-Prussian war and the Commune but he had never before had to hide in his own cellar because war had come to mean bombing planes over Paris!

All this time the cat was making frantic efforts to get out of the oven where we had had to shut it up because it went dashing madly about the cellar. Since there was no other reason for this wildness than some awareness of our state of nerves, we had hoped the warmth of the oven and the seclusion would quiet it. It had air enough too, but the poor creature kept scratching frantically—just as we might be doing if the walls fell in upon us.

We could not understand why the floor sloped so queerly; it was well paved with stone; was the house settling?

The Marquis explained that the clever architect had sloped this floor so that if the water began seeping in from the Seine, during a flood, there would be time to move the wood and the kitchen things upstairs before the water mounted too high.

We were to know something of this ourselves in 1924, but we heard stories of a much worse flood from the Marquis, that of 1910, when the water rose so high in this old rue de Lille that they had had to let down baskets from upper windows for their provisions and their mail, which came in boats along the street.

In the nearby street of St. Dominique, a butcher boy, delivering his meat from a row-boat which he did not really know how to manage, had been drowned in one of the courtyards, like ours, when he tried to turn about to leave the house; and those who were at the upper windows could do nothing to rescue him.

Ghoulish stories, like this one, did not lessen the impression of a world gone mad. We were in no danger from floods; it was not from water but from the air

that the menace reached us. The enemy up in the
clouds, and mankind scuttling down to the cellars!

Fortunately, the military authorities had told us that
no aeroplane could carry more than three bombs at
a time. So, when we heard the first one, we took a
breath and held it until we heard the second. The
Marquis would count: *"Un"* and not another word
until he said: *"deux."* With *"trois,"* we relaxed. *"C'est
fini!"* he would add, and then we would wait when
the last had gone for the bells which would let us
break up this impromptu party.

Whenever a raiding plane was signalled by the siren,
I used to bound from my bed and slip my feet into
black shoes left ready at its side. Then I sprang to the
windows and threw them wide open—no matter how
cold it was outside—for this was the only way to keep
them from being broken by the concussion if a bomb
should fall near us. After that I ran into the hall, shut
the bedroom door behind me, and turned on the light.
Since there was no window from the hall giving on the
street, I could have light.

There, close to the door, on two chairs, were my
clothes—but not my usual clothes, for who could take
time to put on underwear, corsets, boned waists, and
skirts which would have to be fastened? Before me, on
one of the chairs, was the dress which Chanel had invented for war-wear, for night-raids. She had christened
it "the Chemise-dress" and it could be slipped on over

THE AUTHOR'S PARIS HOME DURING THE WAR

Showing the Paper Protectors Pasted to the Windows

the shortened night-dress and be belted later. It had a broad pocket made by the deep hem left open in the front; in this were an undergarment, stockings and garters to be donned when safety was reached—safety, in the cellar.

On the other chair was a small dark hat, and a coat in whose pockets were muffler, gloves, purse and any essentials which had been put in them with the haunting idea that we might not be coming up here again.

Slipping on my dress, seizing my coat and hat, down the two flights of stairs to the cellar!

I could hear the servants opening other windows and slamming doors before they joined us, where the Marquis and his brother could always be counted on to increase our group and diminish our weird sense of isolation.

Once down in the furnace-room, nothing but suspense until the church-bells rang out the news that the raid was over. With the first sound of the bells, silence came to an end and an excited conversation began. It was in one of these social moments that we learned of the Marquis' temerity in leaving four Hubert Robert paintings in his dining-room. We urged him to send them outside of Paris until the war was over. He did.

Sometimes, after a raid, we would, in our relief, join the Marquis and the Count for a short walk around the block to breathe the outer air. Without gas or electricity, the houses in shadow, no lights in the windows, everything hushed, it seemed to me that I had stepped into the Medieval city. On the nights when the moon came out, the scene was as tranquil as could be imagined. Paris belonged to itself again. There was now no haunting enemy up there in the air. The cellar would fade into unreality.

One night, which I recall very vividly, we had scarcely got back to bed after an hour in the cellar, when the siren blew again! With nerves already on edge this second signal seemed to me to mean the end of the world. Two raids in one night! Or had those see-ing-eyes and bombing-hands only made a pretence of withdrawing?

When the church-bells rang out again we were not quite sure that we ought to trust them. Would it not be wiser to stay down here in security, to wait for day-light, to have our breakfast served near the furnace? But habit is strong, and already, in this short space of time, we had acquired the habit of responding both to the siren and the bells, going underground at the first signal, mounting to upper air at the second; and we were soon sleeping peacefully to make up for the hours we had lost.

During the day which followed such a raid, or raids, the stories we heard were not the sort to make us defy the siren when it shrieked again. People talked of the changing size of the bombs; they had, in the beginning, been fairly small and could only do harm on the spot where they fell; but, as the war went on, they were growing and the damage they could do was far greater, as on the night when they released the electric current in the Metro, and all those who had sought safety at the station, called *Combat* (strange coincidence!), were killed because they had crowded out upon the tracks.

After that I never saw those tiny blue lights, which stayed on even during the raids at the entrance of some of the Metros, without shuddering. The word *abri* (refuge) which they lit up had small comfort in it.

Every time a raid was signalled the threat was grimmer than before; no one knew what might happen. That was why, perhaps, on the night between the eleventh and the twelfth of March in 1918, we seemed, all of us, to be keyed up to a higher pitch of anxiety. Or it may have been that we had some premonition of what was to happen so near us.

When the crash came—the loudest and most terrible we had ever heard—the prayers stopped short. No one moved; we were waiting for what was to follow.

Yet the walls did not fall; the light which shone on our white faces did not go out. Only—suddenly—the rushing of water! It sounded like a cataract, louder and louder, until I expected to see it pouring in upon us! We were going to be drowned!

The church-bells rang out at last above the "noise of many waters" but it took more than usual courage to go upstairs. And when we did, and went out into the court to the big door, the noise was still greater: a huge water-main had been opened by the bomb.

It was rather terrifying to find that we could not get that big wooden door open. Behind us, we saw that the windows—which the servants, on this one occasion, had not dared take time to open—were shattered. Fortunately, a smaller door which the Marquis ordinarily used let us reach the disaster.

There, directly in front of the German Embassy next door, as though that seeing-eye in the air had all but measured the distance which would have allowed the bomb to fall upon that house which was the property of the enemy—strange destruction as that would have been—there was a hole much deeper than a man. On its edge, among the blasted stones and earth were lying two silent figures; the two policemen, who had been on guard—as always night and day before all Embassies—had been killed!

Other police and soldiers were already in the street, and as there was nothing that we could do, we went back into the house. It had only suffered in its windows and the long silk curtains in shreds—for knowing how often the salons would have to be left open for hours at a time, during the raids, we had taken all that was precious to us and all the small bric-à-brac upstairs. In the two rooms, where I myself had opened the windows, there was no sign of what had happened out there in front of the house.

As I was closing the windows to shut out that cold night air, the old servant of the Marquis appeared to ask if we had any room which the Marquis might use, as not only had the windows in his bedroom been

BOMB HOLE IN FRONT OF THE GERMAN EMBASSY, PARIS

shivered but his bed was partly shattered. I offered him
the second room; and, after his faithful domestic came
again and again with things which he thought the
Marquis might need, we said goodnight and went to
bed as we had done on other nights when the bombs
had fallen farther afield.

But, as I lay there in the dark, unable to sleep, I
heard the wagon-wheels crunching over the broken
glass in the street. They were coming for the bodies
of those two who had been killed, as by lightning, at
our very door!

In the morning we found the street roped off at
either end of our block. I went out to the policemen
who were already at their posts of duty before the
Embassy.

"You lost two of yours, last night," I said, putting
out my hand.

"Seven, Madame," he replied gravely.

"But can't you, who are of the police, seek a refuge
when there is a raid?" I asked. "Couldn't you come
down into our cellar when there is an *alerte?*"

"We are not allowed to enter any house," he replied,
"unless there is a riot going on, and we are needed."

"Very well," I said. "At the sound of the first siren
remember that there will always be a riot in our
cellar."

There was not a drop of water to be had in the
house. We had to send to a distant fire-hydrant for just
enough to cook with; they did not allow us more. Nor

was there any gas except what we could smell still hanging over the broken main in the street, although it had been turned off. We sent for people to open the great door. They did it, be it said, but then we could not shut it, for something had happened to the hinges. We were sitting in our coats waiting for the glazier to start repairing the windows.

The Marquis had just come from making the regular claim on the authorities for the cost of those repairs— that claim had to be made at once. He was red with indignation; he had heard that the representative of the Germans, those who had the Embassy in their charge, had put in their claims too! I have often wondered if France recognized that claim and paid the enemy for the damage which they themselves had done?

We were still under the effect of the night, sitting in a cold room before a broken window, when Katherine Blake appeared, white and anxious, doubting her eyes when she saw us there.

"But how did you get by the police?" I asked.

"I told them that I was your sister," she replied, "and that I must see for myself whether you were still living."

Katherine, who had been for several years now close to the wounded who were under the care of Dr. Blake at his hospital, knew very well that had we been hurt no news would have been given in the press or by the police: everyone learned at once where the bombs had fallen but the details of their destruction were not made public. The enemy must not know what his success had been; the *moral* of Paris must not suffer by alarming tales which could so easily be exaggerated.

No doubt we took her coming like that as a matter of course, yet what an added effort in a day in which she would be sitting by the beds of her husband's patients, listening to the dying wish of some soldier and carrying it out if there was the slightest chance to do so—no matter how much time it might take or how much money!

No one knows how many railroad tickets she sent to distant villages that mother or father or both might come up to Paris to say good-bye to the boy they had given to France. No one could count the miles she travelled over Paris every day in her mission of mercy, going in person to the mother of someone who had died before his mother could be brought to him, going on to find a daughter of that mother whose presence was needed in some forlorn little flat.

She never spared herself—nor her friends, if they were willing to help. Although she was not a Catholic, she gave half the money to turn a lumber room in the hospital into a chapel, so that the patients who could, might go in to pray and to hear mass. A friend gave the other half of the money needed for the altar, the vestments, the candles, etc.

I remember that a young girl with a lovely voice, a Catholic, was asked to come and sing in the chapel service. She hesitated and came to me for my advice.

"Mrs. Blake has been divorced," she said, "and you know what the Church feels . . ."

"Since she is not a Catholic," I replied, "that divorce does not hurt her conscience, and besides, she has not asked you to sing for *her* but for the wounded."

When Dr. Blake arrived in Paris, he found that all the arrangements had been made for the staff of the American Ambulance Hospital and that he could be on that staff if he wished but under the authority of another. His acknowledged place as a surgeon would not allow that, so he took another hospital under his charge. In fact he had two: one out at Ris Orangis and the other in Paris—so near the Duchess de Talleyrand's big garden that she opened it for those of his patients who could be brought there in their rollchairs. During convalescence, they spent many sunny afternoons among the flowers and fountains of this marvellous garden.

The hospital itself was a model of simplicity and white paint. And how different from the one he found —a private one with carpets and curtains. Under the carpets, when they were taken up, the dirt had actually formed a felt an inch thick; and the curtains were full of antique dust.

"But it will cost so much," said the timid little Sister who had nursed there, "to buy new curtains and carpets for the whole place."

Brown Brothers, photo.

KATHERINE BLAKE, THE FORMER MRS. CLARENCE
MACKAY

"There are not going to be any curtains or carpets," said Dr. Blake.

The hospital at Ris Orangis had been a girls' school until June 1914; then it had been rented, fully furnished, by some Germans. When Dr. Blake went to look it over, he found it perfectly equipped as a hospital. How it had been done without attracting attention, no one knew, but there it was, ready for his French wounded.

The beds and tables and chairs were, of course, already there; the instruments and linen, the bandages and medicine had all been brought, doubtless, in small amounts and inconspicuously. But what was the idea? To have a hospital for the wounded of the victorious Germans.

Yet, lovely as Katherine Blake seemed to us, and devoted as she was to the care of those who needed her, she had relatives right here in France who still sat in judgment upon her for leaving Clarence Mackay and marrying Dr. Blake. How much the thought of his fortune influenced their attitude I do not know, but they certainly insisted upon staying on good terms with Mr. Mackay and they treated Katherine very cavalierly.

Now, these relatives had a house which they called "a château," next door to Fortoiseau, a country house in the Department of the Marne which Dr. Blake had taken; the two gardens adjoined but no one ever

passed through the little gate in the hedge which separated them. Yet there they were, the two families out
in the country—and France at war and the Front so
near!

Before the battle of the Marne saved the day, there
was a good deal of anxiety at the "Château," I remember, as to what might happen. The chatelains,
having heard that the Germans especially liked clocks,
decided to save theirs at all cost; so they took them
all out into the garden and buried them in various
corners.

I hear that they have never gone well since.

Destiny, however, pays small heed to personal dif-
ferences and one of Katherine's relatives had a most
embarrassing encounter with this disregard of the cool-
ness which was being maintained—all on one side—for
Katherine had no feeling of rancor in her.

The relative had established a circle, a sort of school,
for the revival of lace-making, both as a *passe-temps*
for harassed women and as an industrial project. She
was doing a splendid work and we all admired her
tenacity and her talent. But one day, in their old ram-
shackle Tin Lizzie, she started for Paris with all the
materials needed in the enterprise. In the front seat
was the chauffeur and her husband; in the rear, surrounded by all shapes and sizes of packages sat the lady
and her maid. Off they went. But not for any distance;
a big heavy truck, a military lorry, driven too rashly,
ran into them and tore off the front part of the car

with extreme ease—and dashed on. The front seaters, to their great surprise, did not find themselves injured although sitting in a field at some distance from the car, but the lady and maid had been cut by glass and cut about the face and head.

Fortunately another car appeared whose driver seized the relative and maid and ordered her husband to mount up as well, and this great yellow auto did not stop until the anxious driver had deposited the victims at the hospital in Ris Orangis.

Oddly enough everything was in readiness, the necessary stitches could be taken at once, and with the skill for which Dr. Blake was famous. It looked as though Fate had ordered the affair so as to show the relative the manner of man Katherine had married. But she maintained a stoical silence, was distantly polite when the bandages could finally be taken off; there was no change in her attitude.

Some time later, the relative's husband wrote in the third person, begging most formally that Dr. Blake should send his bill.

Dr. Blake, much amused, answered with the same formality—that as he was being paid for his work during the war there would be no bill.

A second formal note from the Château had as enclosure a small sum, a very small sum. The relative did not want to feel under obligation, it seemed. Yet she had to; for on the afternoon of the accident, the ambulance of the Ris Orangis hospital, driven by a charming Jehu whom we all liked immensely, passed the scene of the disaster and seeing packages of all sizes and shapes scattered about—for it was pillow-lace which was under way—and others filling what was left of the car—canes, umbrellas and suit-cases—stopped, took them all aboard and left them—sixteen in number, he told us—in the vestibule of the Château. When the lady returned there was not a thing missing.

I liked the epilogue best of all!

One of the stories which had gone around when Katherine Blake was divorced was that she had given up her magnificent jewels—jewels which had been the talk of New York whenever she appeared in them, for she was one of the women whose beauty brought out whatever was sumptuous and brilliant. So when she arrived at the reception given for President Wilson in Paris, wearing her diamonds—which Mrs. Oelrichs had once said laughingly to her made her look like a walking crystal chandelier—there was a gasp!

Not at the idea of such gems, for it had been agreed that everyone was to wear her best and make the affair as gay as possible for the effect upon our notable guest, but because no one knew that she still possessed them. With that beautiful black hair of hers surmounted by a tiara, which Cartier had said was the handsomest he had ever made, she was the most strikingly beautiful woman present as she walked through the rooms with Dr. Blake.

Later, she took me aside: "I am wearing them," she said, "to show that they were never taken from me. And some night I shall wear my emeralds or my pearls. Then perhaps they will stop talking."

While the party was at its height and, except for the constant conversation touching the war you might have believed yourself in some prosperous kingdom whose happiness was being shared by the crowd which had gathered about the President, the lights began to go out.

There was a quick taking of breath—for it seemed the prelude to something terrible! I was near Dr. Blake at the moment and felt him clutch his wife to him with a gesture of protection which he explained to me afterwards: his first thought had been that the darkness was to be used as a screen to theft. He had been uncomfortable all the evening on her account, for, while he approved of her reason for wearing her jewels, he knew too well that their value was an open secret. Might not someone have planned this way of getting them?

I never saw Katherine Blake wear these jewels again; she may have taken warning from that sudden darkness; she kept them for her children whom she had surrendered to Clarence Mackay, and completely surrendered to him, so that they might not lose the right to his wealth and to the position to which they had been born: two daughters and a son.

It was when the son was born that we all realized

the part which Mr. Mackay's mother played in that house, for it was she who insisted that the boy should have a Catholic baptism. Katherine would not go to the christening. It was easy enough to avoid this as she was not yet quite strong. They asked "Birdie" Vanderbilt to be the godmother and she agreed. But, realizing the situation and not wanting to take sides, she had at the last moment given out and telephoned that ever-ready and cheerful social secretary, Maria de Barril, to take her place.

"You can have the present they were going to make me," she said as an inducement, although she was careful not to give her reason for being suddenly bedridden. And Miss de Barril did not know that she was saving Mrs. Vanderbilt's diplomatic position at the risk of losing her own. It was only after she had accepted the handsome brooch in the form of a diamond horse-shoe—a brooch worthy of a Vanderbilt godmother—that she realized she would never again be called to do anything for young Mrs. Mackay, who had employed her most profitably for several years in all those formalities which have to do with guest lists and details, the chief anxiety of a young matron in New York society.

To Dr. Blake, Katherine gave two other daughters and a son—all of them born in France and born to comparative simplicity, in a home where responsibilities were taken seriously.

Yet I remember when, in that great house of hers

at Harbor Hill, Katherine Mackay was one of those who seemed to live in the moment and to want that moment one of supreme luxury. Mrs. Burke-Roche once told me that when Katherine was showing her the house for the first time—it was not yet completely finished—pointing out the marvellous marble bathroom and the other seven wonders, she had complained as they sat in the boudoir that it was not quite warm.

Like a flash the young hostess had gone to the exquisite writing table—the "secrétaire"—and taking out a drawer full of expensive mauve paper and envelopes, the kind which she always used, had flung them into the open fire-place where they flared into momentary warmth.

"The beggar mounted," commented Mrs. Burke-Roche in that high, distinguished English voice of hers, referring to the aristocratic poverty from which Katherine had married into this luxury.

But I take the other view: that her hostess had an immediate desire to give comfort, and that she did not think of anything but the necessity of having a fire. She was like that—impetuous and self-forgetful.

We used to be amused at her odd ideas of harmony— as for instance that she could not use the red two-cent stamps on her letters because they did not go well with that same orchid-tinted paper. For that reason she used three-cent stamps, which were, perhaps, an extravagance but she doubtless had more than a penny's worth of pleasure when she saw her letters ready to be mailed. And the Post Office profited!

One of her mauve letters made quite a sensation; she wrote to Mrs. Fish, saying that that lady's last note had been so heavily perfumed that she had had to have her butler stand in a strong draft while he read it to her. I do not know how serious she was when she wrote this but I saw the effect upon Mrs. Fish—angry for a moment and then assuming that smile which was hers when a clever idea took possession of her as a *riposte*.

She sent another note to Katherine at once. It was written on a piece of wrapping paper.

When Katherine had written her first book: *The Stone of Destiny*—and a sentimental piece of work it was, even for a sentimental age—and bound in orchid-mauve—she adopted what she considered the right garb for an author: low heels, white shirt-waists, and an utter disregard of her hair—which was, however, so beautiful that it benefited by her negligence. It had always been her boast that neither curling-irons nor curling-papers had touched it; the silky wavy masses of it owed nothing to art.

The dressmakers and the *bottiers* were in despair, for she had been a very profitable customer. Fortunately for them, the mood passed and she had the added charm in their eyes of having come back into the fold when they feared her lost forever to their vanities.

But the thing which, to my mind, makes her story

mount to heroic height was that when she had lost an eye and someone spoke commiseratingly to her of it, she replied, with a courageous smile:

"But think how singly I can now see!"

And it was she who came so quickly that morning after what might have been our last night on earth!

We received her in the windowless room where we were sitting with carriage robes over our knees, but were soon electrified into action, as always, under her influence.

There was a great deal to be done at the American Ambulance and it was there that we were occupied on certain days of the week, while she was in and out of Paris in all weathers for the sake of those who were in Dr. Blake's hospital.

Even the hours of so-called relaxation during these years of the war never really decreased the tension. At the cinema you would hear a woman shriek when she recognized on the screen someone she loved who was there in her sight—but oh! how far away in reality— wounded or dying! Again and again, I saw women leaving with bowed heads, sobbing as they went.

At a luncheon to which James Hazen Hyde had asked several of us, we all determined, at his suggestion, not to speak of the war. We wanted to forget it. But before the second course was served, we were all talking war and disaster.

I recall that at another luncheon someone was describing the effects of being gassed, how after each seizure the result was worse, even though the victim believed himself entirely cured; until under an attack, without warning he would suddenly die. Lady Paget, who had been growing paler and paler, had to be carried from the table; she had fainted. Her son, Bertie Paget, had been gassed several times. He died soon after.

There was no place or time where the war did not give its color to your thoughts. One morning as we came from a service at the Church of the Madeleine, I saw a woman in deep mourning step up to a British officer and say:

"You are in the regiment my son belonged to, may I embrace you?"

Even English diffidence went down under that appeal; and as I passed on I heard her add: "Perhaps you knew him."

No one on the street had any criticism for young soldiers and officers with their arms around their sweethearts, even though the sweethearts might not have been of long acquaintance.

From the very first days of the war, the silence in which most of us go about in public places was of shorter and shorter duration. I remember that Pauline Bassano, early in August 1914, was standing in the Place de la Concorde waiting for an autobus. She had been waiting perhaps a quarter of an hour, not impatiently, because already a new willingness to endure small annoyances had been born, but wondering a little at the delay.

As she leaned to look around, a well-dressed man approached her and lifted his hat.

"Are you waiting for the bus?" he asked.

"I am," she replied, somewhat surprised.

"There won't be any more buses," he said, smiling, "until after the war. They have all gone to the front."

"If he hadn't spoken to me I might have stood there four years," Pauline used to say.

Practical ideas too took on the full glory of ideals in those days. There was Mrs. Whitelaw Reid who never seemed to turn her head without discovering something she could do which would be of practical value. When she remarked that she had never seen hospital cots before with grey blankets and no white spreads, she was told that white spreads could not be afforded. For the money—three hundred thousand dollars—given by Mr. Vanderbilt for the American Ambulance at the beginning of the war, had been spent lavishly with the idea that the war could not possibly last more than two or three months.

"White spreads," said Mrs. Reid, "don't cost a million dollars. I'll send them."

And she did, for the several hundred beds.

"How crowded you are!" said Lady Granard. "Don't you think it would be better to take fewer patients and give them more attention?"

"We have to take all who are brought to us," was

the reply, with some surprise at such advice.

Mrs. Reid, after she had nearly lost her footing in the dimly lighted staircase, asked why they did not have a light. It was because they had no curtains for the windows on the stairs and on the nights of the raids . . .

She sent them.

She gave the hospital two elevators: one for the service and one large enough to accommodate the stretchers. And then there was that little shelter, without a roof, which was used for the office or bureau near the door. For the Lycée Pasteur was just being built when it was handed over for the use of the American Ambulance service and hospital, and a great many things were lacking; it was not even plastered throughout.

The ambulance drivers, with that American ingenuity which does so much in the world, had constructed a makeshift shelter out of old boxes and planks, buying only the hinges and knobs; but it did not reach to the top and it let in the wind. One of the men had died from pneumonia which he contracted while on service in the "shelter."

Mrs. Reid had plain but solid partitions and roof made for the shelter and also an entrance door. When I saw her giving so freely and always the unostentatious necessities, I recalled when I was a child hearing Whitelaw Reid tell my father that at his country place, Ophir Farm, which was near Sing Sing prison, he always kept two old suits of clothes hanging on the side of the barn, close to the road and in full sight of anyone coming along it.

"In that way," he said, with a matter-of-fact air, "I am sure never to be molested by any convict who might be escaping from prison, as their first necessity is a suit of clothes."

Those ambulance drivers have taken their place in romantic tales since the war. They were picturesque as well as courageous; they were full of initiative and they did not lose their sense of humor. Indeed one of them contributed to the amusement of some of us who were careful, however, not to say anything which would hurt him.

It was a young man who bore a world-famous name associated with extreme wealth. He may have been a distant relative, but he had nothing himself of the world's goods which would allow him to play the rôle which he assumed: the rôle of a scion of a great family who, from principle, preferred "to live simply and be liked for himself."

As he was extremely good-looking and had the dashing manner naturally belonging to a care-free youth, he was surrounded by a bevy of pretty women most of the time. It was a harmless game, since only those who hovered about him because they believed him rich would, in the end, be disappointed.

There must have been several, however, who were

seriously disillusioned for when, a few years after the
war, I met his mother and asked how he and the young
wife I had met a year or two before were getting on—
"It was his second wife," I added. She replied:

"Second? Perhaps. He has just married his sixth—at
least, *I think* it is his sixth."

What contrasts there were as part of the everyday
life at the hospital: those formal hours when the
Duchesse de Vendôme would have tea—in a special
cup and saucer—with me, after making her inspection
of the wards. She was the King of Belgium's sister and
was treated with due formality. There were those other
teas on Wednesday, which was my day for supplying
the cakes and sandwiches and giving the hospital something of sociability, although everyone was too busy to
do more than stop a moment.

There were problems which we all gossiped about
without being able to solve them. No one could tell
an officer that his convalescence here had lasted as
long as it could. Ordinarily the beds were evacuated
by general orders; as soon as a soldier could leave, he
had to do so to make room for others in a worse
plight; but the officers, who had rooms apart, always
left on their own initiative, knowing how precious
every bit of space was.

One colonel, however, stayed on. He had had his
arm amputated but he had recovered and was up and
around long since, indeed so much up and around that

THE AUTHOR IN RED CROSS UNIFORM DURING THE WAR

he used his room as though it were a hotel bedroom to sleep in and spent the day in more cheerful surroundings in Paris. Every morning the hospital orderly helped him dress and then he was off—the room standing empty.

No matter how long he might stay on, his arm would not grow again; there was nothing more for the doctors or nurses to do for him, yet everyone hesitated to tell him his room would be more appreciated than his nocturnal company. I think they all realized that he might be clinging to the place as a sort of defence against life—now that he had been maimed; it may have been that he really was afraid to let go this final link with his earlier self. But, in the end, pity for those who needed his bed over-balanced the sympathy we felt for him and he was told to pack up.

Exceptions to rules at the hospital were rare; one rule, for instance, was that no dogs could be brought in. The reason was clear enough and I know of only one exception, made for a beautiful shepherd dog which had saved the life of his master, a Spahi, at the risk of its own and had saved, they said, several other lives. That dog was an honored guest as long as his master stayed and was afterwards decorated.

And the hospital's blackbird! Who, once seeing it walking in front of a funeral procession, could ever forget it? It seemed almost human.

CHAPTER II

PARIS IN WAR TIME

IT WAS HARD FOR AMERICANS, JUST ARRIVED, TO UNDER-stand the mood of Paris and the people—which seemed so calm and yet, in a flash, could lose its good humor, its serenity and tear a boutonnière, taken from a bouquet we had on the table, from the coat of a newly arrived American, swaggering, they felt, a little too nonchalantly in his good clothes, his hat cocked a bit too much to one side. The impatience of the crowd with any sign of indifference spread even to those of us who had been staying on in France with the feeling that to go elsewhere—no matter how little we could help—would be like desertion.

I remember being extremely shocked at a gala given at the Opera for charity, where we were all in dark street clothes, to see a woman come in and take her seat wearing a bright red hat. And I was not the only one to notice her; people actually scowled and looked as though they could tear it from her head.

"What a tactless hat," said André de Fouquières, that arbiter of fashion.

And one day, when we were having tea at the Ritz, in came Mrs. Vincent Astor and a friend, who has since become Mrs. Russell, wearing light blue and pink dresses, with flowers in their hats! It was summer, they had just landed. What they were wearing was simple enough and very pretty—but how the colors jarred on us! We stared at them, first in surprise and then in quite unwarranted indignation.

Dark blue and black were correct at all times and places. I used to remember that woman in New York who came up to Mrs. Fish one evening in the dressing-room before we went in to dinner and said: "How do you like my dress?"

Mrs. Fish considered the black dinner gown before her and said sweetly: "It is just like one I saw in the Opera last night."

"Who was wearing it?" asked the woman, beaming.

"Old Trudel," replied Mrs. Fish, who did not like Opera, "who comes out in the middle of the night and caterwauls in the street."

The Ortrud of the night before had been a particularly blousy sort of villainess and had worn quantities of spectral black in that scene with the fair Elsa in Lohengrin.

When they began to try out smoke-screens and queer gases on the Seine, both of which floated into 80 rue de Lille, the authorities assured us that they were not bad for the health and that it was only their Apocalyptic purpose against the flying dragons which we ought to take into account; but we did yield then to a strong

desire to go where the haunting sense of mysterious
danger could lie dormant for a time.

Because we did not talk much upon the street or in
public places that warning which was to be read on all
the walls and in the Metro, that "enemy ears are listening" had never meant much to us. For that reason we
were surprised to find ourselves, at the end of our
journey, in a place where they were hunting for spies—
or rather for the proof of their recent presence.

And that place, of all places in the world, was Mrs.
Leeds' villa, Primavera at Cap d'Ail—not far from
Monte Carlo—on the French coast. We had only been
there a few days when the police presented themselves
one beautiful morning, "to inspect" it, they said. We
were all a little uncomfortable and Mrs. Leeds was
much upset at this mysterious visit, for not one word
would they say as to why they wanted to inspect the
place.

While we stood about, wondering if there was something which they expected to find among us because
we were foreigners, those men began to work with a
thoroughness which was more than enough to get on
the nerves of the hostess as well as of her guests, so
lately in Paris, and remembering that caution: *"Méfiez-
vous!"*

The police, there were two of them, looked into
every closet, under every staircase, behind every door;
they not only looked at the wainscoting and the mold-
ings with gimlet eyes, and rang bells and turned on

lights, but they took what looked like long hat-pins and stuck them again and again into all the upholstery, into cushions and curtains. And when they had finished with the interior of the big villa, they began to inspect the exterior.

It looked to us as though their search was quite in vain, although of course they might be registering all sorts of suspicious details which escaped us; fascinated, we watched them as they went about looking at the foundations of the villa.

We were up on the porch which faced that unbelievably blue Mediterranean and, had it not been for the disquieting presence of these men, we would have been able to forget the war and the world in looking out at its vast tranquillity. Suddenly there was a flurry of interest almost directly below us. The police asked what this cement pit below the porch had been used for.

"Ah!" said the gardener with a genial smile, "don't you see that this is where the monkey was kept. It was built especially for the monkey."

Very good, the policemen dismissed him and began to measure and write down their figures in their notebooks. Odd, we thought, that they should be so much interested in a monkey-pit! We put a discreet question or two but there was no response, and they bowed themselves off, seemingly well-content with what looked to us like a wasted morning.

Some time later we learned from a very reliable

source that that monkey-pit was also the emplacement of a machine-gun. The owner of the villa was not dead as Mrs. Leeds had supposed when she had signed the lease with his "widow"—he was in the prison at Vincennes, convicted as a spy. He was executed soon afterwards.

Beautiful villas on the Mediterranean were not, it seemed, immune to the war atmosphere.

"What!" said Mrs. Belmont, when I told her of our nights in the cellar. "You went underground? I would rather have been bombed!"

She was not exaggerating, for she had such a fear of anything subterranean that, no matter how it might be disguised as corridor or tunnel lined with lights, she always and everywhere refused to go down into it. I have stood in a hailstorm at Manhattan Transfer, going to New York, waiting for a train which would take us to Jersey City and the ferry because she was afraid of the tunnel. It was the same in Lyons, where she always got out of the train at the Perrache station and, driving through town, regained her train for the South.

One night at Monte Carlo we were dining at the Hotel de Paris and going to the Casino afterwards. When dinner was finished a terrific storm had burst over the place. It need not have bothered us at all because the elevator would take us to an underground corridor between the two buildings and another elevator bring us up into the Casino. Ah, no! Out we went into the pouring rain which had become a cascade, and down the steps of the hotel, in to the carriage to cross the short distance—and up the other great flight of outside stairs!

As for the Simplon or the St. Gothard tunnels—she never saw the inside of those engineering marvels!

Fortunately she was not in Paris during the time of the raids and I must admit that I enjoyed describing to her our sudden descent into the depths of the earth; her feelings about it heightened the effect.

I shall always be glad that I stayed on in Paris until that morning in November 1918 when the whole world was given over to joy because of the armistice! As early as I could, I left the rue de Lille and crossed to the Place de la Concorde. There the two monuments, one to Lille and the other to Strasbourg, were surrounded with the greatest crowds. Lille, occupied since 1914, was free; the funeral wreaths could be taken from the heroic statue of a woman which represents that city in Flanders.

As for Strasbourg, the black mourning veil which had been upon it since 1870—and which, badly beaten down by the rains, was in her lap under the funeral wreaths—was to be taken off this morning and given in small pieces to those who had helped to regain Alsace. The American soldiers were the first to be allotted these little black souvenirs of the French sorrow turned to joy.

To see better what was going on, I clambered—with

the help of an American soldier—up on a gun from
Arras. Here I clung and waved my American flag as
though my life depended upon it. And the American
soldier next me waved his.

"Why are you waving a Chinese flag?" I shouted into
his ear, for the noise of jubilation and military music
was deafening.

"I didn't know it was Chinese," he shouted back.
"It was the last flag in the shop so I took it." And he
kept on waving.

The crowd was souvenir mad; it had already taken
everything it could from the captured aeroplanes,
which were up on the Tuileries terraces; it was tear-
ing loose what it could from the guns. Some ardent
collectors were taking the guns themselves. You met
them all over Paris; drivers had to turn out to let them
pass. It was genial pillaging. Near my house, in front
of a popular café on the Boulevard St. Germain, there
had been hauled a big gun and with a young woman
sitting proudly upon it!

"Let the children play with them," said General
Gallieni, the Military Governor of Paris. "We have
plenty more."

Next door to my house, the heads of the two German eagles, which had been put on top of the great
gate by the King of Prussia, had their heads tied up in
red, white and blue bunting.

"How times have changed," Count Antoine used to
say when we were having one of our reunions below

stairs. "How unlike the calm nights of my childhood in Paris."

And that recalled to me that I, too, had known Paris as a child. My sense of the contrast was but little less vivid than his. For when we first stopped at the Hotel Meurice we had found the nights calm and quiet when we went upstairs—on foot and not in an elevator—and serenely lighted by lamps and candles.

In those days my father used to take his coffee at a table in the courtyard under a big and gay umbrella while he read his paper; the fiacres with their yellow wheels, their buff-colored coachmen in white top hats, the horse wearing a bell, used to come rattling into the court over the stone cobbles. And, as I told the Count, on a recent night when we had been in our cellar, a man we knew, stopping at the Meurice, had been in that courtyard now transformed into the Palm Garden, and hearing the siren had found himself, an instant later, hiding under a table! As though a table would be any protection!

CHAPTER III

SARATOGA: THE PIAZZA

BUT I MUST ADMIT THAT, WITH ALL ITS FOREIGN SMART-
ness, the Meurice had not impressed me as much as the
Hotel United States at Saratoga which I had visited
before coming to Europe. Even today that first impression of its magnificence, lifting the roof of its piazza
three stories high, still occupies a place in my memory
unlike any other.

To think that those slender columns—they were in
pairs upon narrow bases—could support that roof so
high above our heads with its pale blue ceiling! A pale
blue ceiling out-of-doors!

The floors of both piazzas were painted a battle-ship
grey and so were the stairs which seemed to pour
from the front one with grandeur down to the street.
The newel posts held, one a young Indian brave, the
other an Indian maiden, clasping enormous candelab-
ras with many glass globes.

Society sat enthroned upon that piazza on the
garden! For the "United States" was the last word in
elegance and the piazza was an immensely long open-
air Peacock Alley; it ran parallel to the Blue Parlor
and the two smaller parlors, turned at right angles and

Brown Brothers, photo.

THE GRAND UNION HOTEL, SARATOGA

ran the length of the dining-room. There was room upon it for those one thousand guests which the "United States" boasted it could accommodate—without taking account of such entries as that famous one: "William K. Vanderbilt, wife, two maids, two dogs, and fifteen horses!"

The Vanderbilts had come here for the first time when they were on their honeymoon, as Mrs. Belmont told me years later, and had one of that row of hotel cottages which faced the dining-room wing and made the third side of the garden in whose center was the pavilion for the band.

The fourth side was fenced, and the railroad track sliced off an angle so that the garden was not a perfect quadrangle. The noise of the trains which sometimes passed when the music was playing in the morning or when it was playing for the "hops," on Saturday evenings, did not seem to distress anyone; it was too closely associated with the Goulds and the Vanderbilts and other rich men who were coming to Saratoga because they had so profitably established such railroads all over America.

The sight of the trains crossing slantwise the very street upon which the "United States" and the "Grand Union" hotels were built was part of Saratoga's attraction. The railroad cut the principal street into Broadway and North Broadway where our house was. Heads hung out of every window of the trains, in order to see the wealth and fashion of the Queen of Spas, as they passed through town. On any afternoon there was a good deal of it to be seen in the fine "turn-outs," whose prancing horses added to the picture through which the wide-eyed faces flashed.

The piazza afforded me my first social pageant and what an impression it made upon me; two rows of chairs—grouped around tables—among them the famous cane-rockers—filled with women wearing the most marvellous clothes and careful, if they did not boast an escort, to have their crocheting or their embroidery to occupy them in a lady-like way.

For whatever lace and silk fluttered up and down in the promenade, while music played from eleven to twelve every morning, must be visibly attached to a gentleman in striped trousers and neatly buttoned coat, surmounted by a top hat, carrying a cane and wearing or carrying gloves!

If that escort was not possible, the costume must be shown from a chair on one or the other side of the piazza (which was more than twenty feet wide).

Decorous conversation went on uninterruptedly while the music played; the promenaders walked very slowly, aware of the appraising looks fixed upon them by those who were on the side lines. Some of the ladies wore gloves, too, and carried parasols. That parasol must match the gown. Gloves must have been most uncomfortable on August mornings, but—

"No lady," said my mother, "thinks of going out

without gloves."

And the question which echoed every day at least once in the morning and once in the afternoon, as we were ready to issue forth:

"You are sure you have your gloves, Bessie?"

What man today would walk up and down a piazza for an hour before lunch in July and August, or even in September, dressed as Captain Beach or Lispenard Stewart used to be? What woman would spend from breakfast until eleven o'clock dressing for that fashion show?

If a man had no lady of his own, or preferred to shine alone during the promenade, he would, hat in hand, move from one group to another to chat. But woe to the woman who buzzed from group to group! She was considered "bold"—she was accused of wanting to show off her clothes.

No wonder the Saratoga trunk became an institution! It took two stout men to carry it. When it was to be packed there were quantities of tissue paper lying alongside, to be stuffed into sleeves and boned collars and "busts." The bows of ribbon, too, had to be filled out with tissue paper; the one great anxiety was that the clothes would be irreparably crushed!

All this effort for the sake of running the gauntlet upon that piazza by day and in dining-room and ballroom by night. Years later one of my sisters went to the "United States" out of season and wrote us that it was the first time she had ever walked down the piazza without her knees trembling. Few of the "lady guests" would have been so frank but I am sure that if we could have looked beneath that air of unconsciousness, that nonchalant manner which most of them managed to assume, we would have seen the quaking knee above the trimly shod foot which trod that august board.

There was one notable exception, Helen Hamersley, who always ordered her phaeton to be at the little door on Division Street during the music hour. The Hamersleys had the first of the cottages in that row which belonged to the hotel. From her piazza, Miss Hamersley gained the big one whose whole length she walked, carrying with pride, a whip which she cherished because of its make and its beautiful handle. It was an English whip and was never left in the carriage but brought back with the same impressiveness to repose in the cottage umbrella-stand.

The passage of Miss Hamersley, who dressed extremely well—and whose H.R.H. on her handbag was always noted—became a daily ceremony to which the piazza looked forward with interest. She went out again in the afternoon, for having six horses at Saratoga, they must be exercised—one season six black ones, so much alike that it looked as if one pair was being driven morning, noon, and night.

"They must think us very cruel, if they imagine we have but one pair of horses," said Miss Hamersley.

But most of those who brought their horses to Saratoga, or engaged them there for the season, drove only in the afternoon, when "turn-out" after "turn-out" came up to the door and gathered in its customary occupants, the disengaged looking on.

And off for Moon's!

Moon's was four miles from the hotel, out on Saratoga Lake. There was no mistaking the place, for the proprietor had had painted upon the carriage shed a large moon (followed by " 'S") emerging from rather startling clouds and underneath, "Lake House and Steamboat Landing." This same device he had printed upon the little squares of paper which were twisted with a flourish into cornucopias before your eyes when you stopped your carriage—as you always did—to get some of Moon's browned crisp potato chips; "Moon's potatoes" they were called by those who came out here for them, but "Saratoga chips" to the rest of the world!

Saratoga was a "Spa" but some of her fame rested solidly upon the trunk named for her and was upheld —is upheld even today—wherever Moon's potatoes are appreciated.

There was of course the beauty of the Lake and of the country-side for attraction, and there were the big places along the drive. Mrs. Frank Leslie's was the best known at this time, partly because it was next to Moon's and could be looked at as the horses slowed down to stop in front of the cheering odor of the chips.

We had our ponies, my sister and I, and mother had one of those small phaetons with the delightful fringe hanging from the cream-colored top. This she herself drove in the mornings when she did not care to go horse-back riding. In the afternoons we drove, by turns, with mother in the victoria to the Lake.

One summer, a very serious Englishman was visiting us at Saratoga; he had come over, he told my mother, to study American grains and cereals for a book he was writing. Mother thought he ought to see them in the country round about Saratoga and took him to drive with her in her phaeton.

Now, she did not know the difference between corn, wheat, rye and oats, but she had learned that buckwheat was not grown in England. So whenever her companion asked what any field of growing grain was, she felt certain that it was none of the grains he could recognize; for that reason alone it must be buckwheat, and she told him blithely that it *was* buckwheat.

After he had pointed out different fields, no two of which were at all alike and she had told him they were fields of buckwheat, he said timidly: "But they all look so different, Mrs. Drexel."

"Of course they do," she replied, serenely, "they are fields of buckwheat in different stages of growth."

Afterwards her conscience pricked her: ought the English-reading public be made to believe that little else than buckwheat could grow around Saratoga?

Of the thousands who came to Saratoga, I suppose there were a few who really came to drink the water, but I never heard those long hours of discussion about the different treatments and their success which you

hear at most watering-places. Today, no doubt, Saratoga has worked out all the "cures" in modern fashion,
but when I was a child the drinking of the water was
rather desultory. There was "High Rock" and "Red
Star" and a certain sulphur spring at which my mother
would occasionally dismount from her horse to taste
with a wry face. But the "Congress Spring" which was
near the Grand Union Hotel had the greatest number
of frequenters because of the Park which was behind
it, in which one strolled with an elegant and leisurely
air.

My father, I recall, took the baths at "Magnetic
Spring" but he did not spend much time in the usual
Saratoga killing-of-time; he was interested in astron-
omy and had built, in an empty lot close to our house,
a tower in which to have his telescope; here, as in New
York, he spent much time star-gazing—to the amazement of the native villagers.

While my mother was a romantic sort of person, she
did not occupy much time with the stars; her concern
one season was to have a lamb on the green lawn in
front of the house. The lamb had to be very white and
woolly and to be wearing a blue ribbon. It must have
been rather hard on the lamb to be compelled to gam-
bol all alone, but my mother did not think of that, nor
was she at all moved when, at the end of the summer,
it was led away to be transformed into roast lamb and
chops by the butcher to whom she had given it.

Later, when she had grounds which ran down to the

Delaware River at Pen Rhyn, peacocks appeared, and not being edible—except to ancient Romans—were kept from season to season. Indeed the birds might have lived out their noisy existence had not peacock-feathers come into fashion for millinery. When the birds disappeared, my mother thought it was for hats!

Even the name of our house at Saratoga expressed her bucolic affection. After much thought she decided to call it "Robins' Roost," as there were a great many robins about. She ordered robins'-egg-blue letter-paper with several robins in color sitting on a branch of apple blossoms. She never doubted the choice of name until a foreign visitor, an Italian, writing to her after his departure, addressed his letter to "Robinson's Roast."

What four-in-hands there were! What coaches! What ladders to descend by! What ruffled petticoats in descending! A fanfare to rouse your interest every time a coach arrived!

For, although horse-racing was the great and constant attraction of Saratoga, the annual regatta was the most important of the Saratoga events. For there was a perfect straightaway course of three miles on the Lake, wide enough for eight sculls abreast.

To hold the crowds which came out along Union Avenue by coach and carriage and by that little horse-car whose tracks were to one side between two rows of fine trees, there had been a grand stand put up in front of Moon's. The sheds for the coaches and carriages

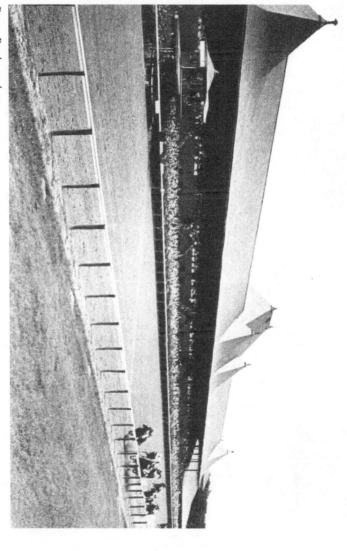

Brown Brothers, photo.

THE RACE TRACK AT SARATOGA

were big affairs and the hitching-posts, which were little Negro jockeys in painted iron, occupied the foreground.

The regatta allowed society to show off its clothes and its horses as the opening "event" of the day. Ladies climbing to their places on the grand stand were sure of being seen to advantage. Yet some of them felt that it was more distinguished to have their seats on Moon's piazza which overlooked the Lake; above the stand it was so delightfully "rustic" too, something in the way of a Petit Trianon for the queens of Saratoga.

Lace gowns, however, in place of Marie Antoinette's simpler muslin. My mother preferred foulards, she said, and wore them. I was much impressed by the fact that, for coaching, her parasols were "tailored"—flowers, perhaps, painted upon them, but no flounces or bows. And the simplest of handles, not even bearing the incrusted ten-dollar gold-piece which she had on a flounced parasol as a protest against the too ornate handles of other ladies who frequented the Piazza.

With what dismay, what horror even, that overdressed and bejewelled crowd would have glazed upon their successors at later Saratoga regattas wearing "sports clothes." At that time they had never been heard of, unless in connection with hunting, and even hunting costumes were never referred to under that heading for the simple reason that it had not yet been coined. There was a regatta every season to which the fashion of Saratoga would hasten out on that same

Union Avenue—one of the finest I have ever seen, with four rows of trees. The prophecy proved true which was made in an old copy of *Harper's* that I came across the other day; it was dated 1876 and read: "Saratoga will ever be the resort of wealth, intelligence and fashion."

Yet, unsuspected, the era of sports clothes was close at hand; the blazer was to bring it in for men—a mild beginning—the sailor hat and shirtwaist for women. It came in with lawn tennis. And the earliest habitat of tennis at Saratoga was, in spite of the connotation so contradictory in the name itself, at "Nestledown," the cottage of the Misses Sands out on Geyser Road.

Great was the interest in the announcement that the Misses Sands had had a tennis court laid out on their grounds.

"People are playing tennis in England," said Miss Sands in explanation of their daring.

They made a point of inviting guests to come to watch the games on Saturday mornings, but all week long everyone went driving by to catch a glimpse of the young ladies playing upon the green; for tennis courts had not become billiard tables as to smoothness, nor were they of Pompeian red. As yet, the most important item was the net; racquets and balls were two other essentials but not matters for expert pondering as to form and material. Although I do recall that Miss Lathrop, who lived next door to us, used to boast of her English racquet: "Mine's a Daft," she would say with the air of Helen Hamersley carrying her English whip. As for that frame, in which the racquet was to be conserved when not in use, that had not been invented.

I do not see how those who sat about the courts to watch the play on Saturday mornings could have kept from wild laughter: picture the Misses Sands and their partners in shirtwaists, with high boned collars, with cravats held in place by big brooches. I recall that one of the Misses Sands wore a pin with "Roma" done in mosaic. Spotted veils dropped from sailor hats, pinned atop the plentitude of hair. (Ah! what a loss of metal hairpins all over the court!)

The sleeves of the waist came down to the wrist and were tight at that point, no matter how they might be enlarged higher up the arm. The belt, too, was tight around a waist well corsetted for the sake of the fashionable hour-glass figure. The full-pleated skirt, with a small bustle—oh, just a *soupçon* of a bustle on the tennis court—came down to the ground. It had to be held up—not an easy accomplishment—in order not to trip over it when running after the ball.

At the best, the speed was not great, but why should it be? They were not playing for championships but for pleasure, or, it may be, for the sake of doing what was being done in England.

The men played in blazers of brilliant stripes—upon their heads the inevitable jockey caps made of the same material. The name of that insouciant jacket came from "blazon," for they had been worn first in friendly student tourneys at Oxford and Cambridge. At the beginning of its career in America, the colors had to be those of the college: the crimson and black of Harvard, the yellow and black of Princeton, the white and blue of Yale, the light blue and white of Columbia, etc.

The arrival of sports clothes upon the horizon was really more than a dawning, it was a vivid outburst of splendor—at least for the young men.

CHAPTER IV

THE BLUE PARLOR

THERE WAS A LONG MIRROR AT THE END OF THE BLUE parlor of the "United States," and one of the first memories I have of the hotel was coming in one morning through the double doors at its other end and walking towards myself for a distance of nearly ninety feet. How small I was in that immensity!

I looked neither to the right nor to the left, where, symmetrically arranged were the groups of chairs—most of them upholstered in the color which gave its name to the parlor—a table in the center of each group. The high windows were framed with the blue lambrequins and side curtains and, although they looked out on the two piazzas, they had the usual Nottingham lace curtains whose edges were outlined with white tape. The blue-patterned carpet was magnificently Victorian.

Blue parlor indeed! Even the foundation satin of the two enormous screens in teakwood frames, which stood on either side of the great mirror, and which were much scrutinized by admiring ladies because of the oriental embroidery,—even they were deep baby blue.

Above me, at fifteen foot intervals, were five enormous chandeliers with many round white globes whose
every gas-jet contributed its quota of perfume and
added to the attractions of the band in the morning.
And so great is the power of association that today I
never catch a whiff of escaping gas without a pleasant
sense of "Society" at its refulgent best. . . .

Never before in my young life had I seen so many
people eating together as in the dining-room of that
hotel which could seat a thousand. The small tables
were in four rows, two on each side of the main aisle,
broad enough for a parade. And never before or since
have I seen dark-hued waiters slide with such exquisite
precision from the door to the tables, with their large
trays held high, and made higher by tiers of carefully
balanced small platters and "bird bathtubs." For the
"United States," which easily held its supremacy above
all the other hotels at Saratoga and ranked with the
best in New York, used dishes and silver whose qualities were solid and substantial but far from dainty. The
morning coffee cups were heavy to lift, and awkward
to hold because of the thick handles.

But no one thought of complaining; "staying at a
hotel" did not mean then what it does today in the
way either of comfort or luxury. For the Vanderbilts
and the Goulds the "United States" was a matter of
course during the Saratoga season. Mr. Vanderbilt always had the same table and it was on the main aisle.
Many of the ladies preferred to be on that aisle rather

Brown Brothers, photo.

STARTING FOR THE RACES, SARATOGA

than in more retired places near the windows; they could see the coming and going of the guests and note what each one was wearing. Clothes played an acceptedly conspicuous rôle, occupying the attention in a way they could not possibly do today, under any circumstances.

Helen Hamersley, who was always so beautifully dressed and so very self-possessed as she walked under the fixed gaze of the Piazza, became, in my eyes, a model of elegance. On Sundays, instead of crossing the piazza and going out the side-door which was near the Bethsaida Church—which we attended too—she would float down the great front steps of the "United States" and walk with downcast eyes along Broadway to the corner, prayer book in hand. She used to wear to church a sort of Tudor bonnet made of white lace, which I found immensely becoming, a grey dress with flounces and a black velvet shoulder cape with peaked shoulders.

In New York she and her sister, Mrs. Courtland Bishop, had their gowns made at Weatherley's, the English tailor; when, at the same hour every day, they emerged from her house at 255 Fifth Avenue, for their walk, they would be dressed exactly alike. It always created a sensation, even though, like some subterranean court bulletin, the news had leaked out as to what they were going to wear that day.

Such pre-news would have been explainable at Saratoga where, very often, the ladies were approached before some big affair and asked point blank what their gowns would be like, and what jewels they were going to wear. I remember that Mr. Smith, the head usher at the "United States," was deeply grieved, not to say indignant, when my mother changed her mind on one occasion and wore, not the pink gown she had said she would, but a white one.

—If women were going to change their minds like that, would the society reporter, who depended so confidently upon him, be able to send off her account of the Saratoga happenings before they took place?—

In New York Miss Hamersley always appeared, on a cold day, wearing a very thick veil—and doubled at that—for the sake of her complexion:

"I couldn't do this in Paris," she would say, "it would be misunderstood; they would think I was going to a rendezvous."

That complexion was helped out with the most delicate make-up; and I thought it the height of distinction that she should daintily rub her chosen perfume behind her ears in order not to disturb her complexion's smoothness. That made more impression, I am afraid, than the fact that she always had a Bible class at Cottage Number One on Sunday afternoons, and that she was one of the founders of the "King's Daughters."

Mr. Joseph Smith, who was the combined Master of Ceremonies and Bouncer of the "United States," had his office under the great staircase in the entrance hall. He was consulted there upon all occasions where his experience was needed. Sometimes he leaped forth from his desk to greet a guest whom he considered worthy of special attention. That attention depended upon 'he wealth or social importance of the guest.

Knowing this and having been one of the favored guests, Captain Beach, one of our friends, was not surprised to find that in the *Reminiscences of Saratoga,* which Mr. Smith had written, he himself was spoken of as coming "honestly by the military title" he bore, and was "as fine a gentleman as ever visited the Spa."

But, he was startled by the statement of Mr. Smith who, after speaking kindly of the guests of the "United States," wrote: "I received from them nothing but the most considerate kindness."

"Indeed?" ejaculated Captain Beach—"What about our tips?"

The author of the *Reminiscences* preferred never to speak of money except as "finance"—"high" if possible. He enjoyed looking at the men and women about him with a certain air of condescension which delighted most of his readers who knew his real rôle at the hotel and had always played up to it.

Another great friend of my mother came in for a description which may or may not have pleased him: "Mr. Johnson," writes Mr. Smith, "is a typical gentleman of the old school. Always wearing a stiff stock and stand-up collar, with shirt front of the finest and whitest linen, a tall glossy tile, a black broadcloth frock-coat, deep-skirted and closely buttoned over a pair of the darkest and finest cassimere pants (!), his costume as a whole was certainly very respectable and aristocratic and dazzled younger men into a deference which youth rarely shows in these days either to age or position."

But, there was a note of gentle reproof in Mr. Smith's description of the "tall florid man from Texas who was flaunting his hand about as he drank his Hathorn water at the Spring. There were three diamond rings on the hand that held the glass. His necktie of white satin had a scarf-pin of a diamond and a dark blue sapphire, and this was pulled down to show an immense solitaire which served as a collar button."

Youth is not mentioned as being full of deference for the man from Texas but I have no doubt, even though Mr. Smith might not have approved, that whatever youth was drinking Hathorn water that morning it admired the collar button.

Another one of the guests—although a perfectly proper *pater familias*—was granted the doubtful encomium of being "straight as an arrow and strong as a satyr."

But Mr. Smith, as head of a staff of efficient ushers, had acquired a mastery of the art of ridding the "millionaires' piazza," as he called it, of those who came and pre-empted the best of the cane rockers or leaned artistically upon the balustrade without having first

written their name in the golden book which was to
serve as the basis of his memoirs. The Piazza must be
kept pure. And it had, occasionally, to be purified—but
without any sort of disturbing scene. At first, he con-
fesses, he used to ask the interlopers if they were "staying" at the hotel. As that was an ambiguous question,
since they were certainly staying there at the moment,
and could say so without flickering an eyelash, he
finally became direct and asked a more embarrassing
question: the number of their room?

What hotel would you find today, even in the most
modest "resort" which would have a ball-room with
absolutely white walls and no curtains at the windows,
nothing at all for decoration but those fearful chandeliers with their death-dealing light?

Yet the Saturday evening "hops" were looked forward to as occasions for the display of charm and costume, certain to hold their own—their possessors assumed—even under the blaze from the white globes.
As for dancing, when the women carried so many
pounds of clothes, it was a *tour de force* which spoke
well for their physical stamina. My mother, however,
was once so exasperated by the weight of a new skirt
which had just come home from Redfern's that she
ordered a butcher's scales to be brought into her
dressing-room: the skirt weighed eleven pounds! She
sent it back—her doctor, she said, had advised against
wearing such heavy skirts when out for exercise.

What hotel today would have been proud—as Mr.

Smith insists—upon the look of the dining-tables set for their hundreds, where down the whole length of four rows of tables the points of the intricately folded napkins appeared above the rim of tall goblets, and from other goblets, still taller, waved the green foliage of celery?

Think what has happened to celery since those days: it lies flat, delicately denuded of all but an ivory-tinted leaf of two. The napkins, as well, have fallen and are obsequiously flat and square.

Yet, the proprietors of the "United States" did have a care for intimacy; when the season began to come slowly to an end, with the gathering chill of the late September days, the great dining-room had a way of shrinking which kept its guests from noting any vast empty spaces left by those who had departed. Huge rose-coloured screens began to descend from the upper end, pushed a little more each day, to hide the tables where so lately had echoed rippling laughter and clashing bird bathtubs.

The cottages would close day by day, and at "Robins' Roost," we would be occupied in packing the Saratoga trunks for our flight—a heavy one—towards New York. One "season" was over, another was about to begin. For me the coming one was announced by the putting of rubber mats upon the stone steps of our house on Madison Avenue and the starting of the furnace. Winter would be heralded some morning by a hummocky ridge of snow along either edge of the sidewalk. It was a matter of interest to me that Fifth Avenue only had one ridge down the middle, while Madison Avenue had two, one next each curb.

CHAPTER V

103 MADISON AVENUE

AT SARATOGA WE HAD BEEN ALLOWED OCCASIONALLY, in white muslin and sashes, to look on at a Saturday evening hop; in New York we were to return to study and to watching the life of society from the higher regions—that is to say, from our own third-floor where my sisters and I had our rooms. Our house on Madison Avenue was one of the very few large ones in New York at that time, and after I grew up, my father joined it to 25 East 29th Street, round the corner, thereby adding three more large salons to the two we already had.

We could go into mother's room where the guests were taking off their wraps before going down to the dinner from which we were excluded because of our youth. Indeed it was usual for us to have our dinner upstairs by ourselves, except on Sundays. But we always participated in the excitement of preparation, when the drugget was taken off the dining-room carpet and the slip-cover from the embroidered chair in mother's room, when the flowers came from the florist's and had to be arranged for the dining-table and the drawing-room.

And crowning glory! at the last moment before the guests arrived, the two bronze dragons over the door of our blue drawing-room were lighted and were seen to be spitting fire at each other! A quaint device whose inventor should have been there to see the effect he had achieved—particularly upon me. This was the Age of Gas. That was indeed a wonderful invention, when it arrived, which allowed all the lights in the parlor to be turned on at once, later in the Electric Age.

At the Metropolitan there were gas-jets, below all the boxes of the Diamond Horseshoe, arranged in sets of five with white frosted globes. Sometimes when they were turned down too low during an act, they would go out. The smell of escaping gas would be noted quickly; the liveried gas-lighter soon appeared in the darkness at the back of the box, gently inserted himself between bejewelled ladies, leaned over and re-lighted the gas as noiselessly as possible. I found this very diverting if it happened at some Saturday matinée when, against my will, I had been taken to hear music for which I had no taste; although the gorgeous settings of the operas entranced me.

But the most romantic of all social events to my eyes —and solely to my eyes—since I never participated in them—were the luncheon parties which my mother used to give. For, no matter what the season or the weather, daylight was shut out. The more artificial the light the better, so the window curtains were drawn close and pink shades put around the gas globes and over the candles.

Into this gentle glow came the guests, chattering and cooing, impressed by the fact that day had been transformed into night and night so becomingly lighted up. The contrast with the turning of night into day, as at the ball, did in time penetrate the social consciousness of those who gave parties, and the practice of pink shades, or their equivalents, was extended, much to the added beauty of both costumes and complexions.

Druggets! You never see them any more. I doubt if the younger generation even knows what they are. Yet they served to save fine rugs in dining-rooms, preserving them from stains. Of indeterminate colour, sometimes with printed patterns, occasionally with a design of their own, they were light enough to be taken up and shaken frequently; the carpets themselves never coming up more than once a year. How I hated a grey and brown Brussels carpet which my mother had chosen for its very neutrality as a background for her pink bedroom, because a pink one, she said, was impossible!

We had two Aubusson carpets which pleased me, and there were certain Gobelin tapestries brought back from Europe (which had been made to fit the blue drawing-room chairs of ebon framework) for which I felt respect, because they were decorated with Aesop's fables. I did not notice, nor did anyone else, that they had a setting in this New World, to which they had come, which would have astonished the Gobelins' director himself. The most striking part of that setting was, however, the old-world lambrequin. It was everywhere. It had descended so many centuries before from the helmet of the knight to become an essential in the "dressing" of window and door that few guessed its origin. It was put up to hide honest woodwork, to act as dust-gathering cornice, with woollen fringe and tassels.

Yet the day came when they were deposed from our house—all of them except the spinach-green set in my father's study, next the rooms where we used to be allowed to sit with him and my mother the evenings when they dined alone at home. The warm, affectionate memory of that room is framed in green lambrequins. The other lambrequins had to make way for ruffles whose purpose, however, was not far different since they were put up to hide the rings on curtain rods. I remember watching my mother sew rings, innumerable rings, on the new curtains which marked this change in fashion.

She liked to sew—occasionally. One of her favorite occupations was making that crazy quilt—which was to be sold at a Charity Bazaar—out of odd pieces of silk and the ribbons which had been worn by committees at Charity Balls. The dates of the balls were stamped on them; mother, choosing a hexagonal pattern for the quilts, had the die for cutting the pieces made at Tiffany's.

Such an odd mingling of simplicity and super-luxury, a veritable allegory worked out in crazy-quilt fashion. Simplicity was borne in upon me and my sisters, for our third floor was a sort of cocoon stage so far as interior decoration went. We did not have lace curtains at our windows: sash-curtains were all that were deemed essential. There was only one bathroom for the floor and one clock. There was, in reality, only one chair besides the rocker for the nurse; we sat on stools—three-legged stools without backs because our mother had determined we should all be straight and not loll.

This discipline made sitting on the high Elizabethan chairs at Sunday dinner an event. My mother had chosen those chairs, and to me they seemed thrones. But my father found the backs too high; the butler had difficulty in serving us. He finally persuaded her to let him change them and sent home a set of honest-to-goodness dining-room chairs with leather seats and backs, keeping the two "theme-chairs" for himself and my mother. My mother sighed whenever she looked at them—"just ordinary chairs!"

When, later, we were allowed to come downstairs for breakfast, that dining-room—with the sun streaming through the east window, a fire on the hearth—seemed to me heavenly. On the mantel were two alabaster vases in the form of ewers which my father had bought on his honeymoon at Florence. Between them was the cellaret, on the front of whose box was a Wedgwood plaque with cupids and roses. On a rack

in front of the fire was the morning paper which the
butler had put there to dry out. And on the other side
of the fireplace was the plate-warmer, of tin or sheet-
iron, its three sides painted a soft green with roses
upon it. Each one of us coming in for breakfast would
take out a plate from the pile warming on the shelves.

With the decoration of that room I shall never have
any fault to find.

Nearly all the details of the two periods, then and
now, are in contrast, the dust-pan in those days, the
vacuum cleaner today, damp tea-leaves upon the Brussels carpets and a silent broom, where now there is the
ron-ron of a motor. Housekeeping has become household "economy."

There were no marble bathrooms with sunken tubs
and frescos; we considered the bathroom on the second
floor to be a model of luxury because of the mahogany
rim around the zinc tub; it was quite an innovation
when a second bathroom was installed for my father
in his dressing-room. As for the guest-room bathroom,
it held a stationary washstand with slender spigots
arched most uncompromisingly, like protecting spirits,
over the round basin. But three bathrooms on one
floor were remarkable in any New York house even
the size of ours.

Furniture was not added without due forethought
as to where it was to be placed and what other pieces
must yield a favored position and retreat to more
modest surroundings, but bric-à-brac was added in-

continently, as long as there was a place "on the top of the book-case." No one ever seemed to notice the incongruity of such a pedestal for that Saxe coach and four horses which my mother had lost her heart to—and had sent home one day.

Then there were the two silver vases which had made their appeal to her but which her conscience would not allow her to buy for herself—"I'll give them to Joe for Christmas," she said, and paid for them.

But my father thought them awful and told her so frankly, whereupon, dropping subterfuge, she admitted: "I wanted them to put those yellow wax roses in."

The climax of the period, however, was the acceptance of Eastlake chairs and tables which, more or less of bamboo and more or less gilded, were the last word in fashionable furniture. Sir Charles Eastlake had had the happy idea of searching out medieval designs for modern furniture; the results of his efforts, I am sure, went far beyond his expectation. He had rendered people like my mother "furniture-conscious."

"Periods" had begun!

That aspect of social life which was figured in the simplicity of Mrs. Astor who liked old-fashioned things and clung to them, who consciously stood for the formalities and dignities, underwent a transformation immediately after her death and faded almost completely by the time the war came.

At Mrs. Astor's you would have recognized the place

had you been introduced into the drawing-room or the ball-room after years of absence; the curtains and carpets and chairs would all have looked the same even though they had been changed several times. But, after 1900, "periods" began which could be recognized even by those who made no pretence of being interior decorators. The Louis styles for French and the English Elizabethan.

Then there was the Trellis! The trellis appeared in the most remarkable places, wherever it could catch the dust—all the dust except that of the garden which alone would not have given offence. There were square trellises and lozenge-shaped ones; they were extended upon impossible walls. They broke the one great rule of decoration: they were never where they could serve the use for which the trellis was conceived!

The period of the Yellow Bowl followed, a comparatively innocent insistence upon the importance of that bowl in the center of your dining-table, or somewhere in the room where the "effect" was what the decorator desired.

After that it was the Black Curtain, a sinister development suggesting the influence of some devil's mass upon impressionable persons who then went into the decorating art as an outlet to their emotions. But as there is no state of rest in a period of art, the Black Curtain—and black carpets whose seams always wore white—had to give way to something.

To what?

To the Sarcophagus. It was wonderful to see to how many uses a "Roman" sarcophagus could be put, other than the one for which it was designed. It made an excellent aquarium; or it could be made part of an indoor fountain with a mask—not necessarily a death-mask—above it for the water to trickle from.

Reaction set in, as might be expected: the gloom of association with sarcophagi—even when authentic—had to yield to the gaiety of soup-tureens. The soup-tureen has not been explained to my entire satisfaction, particularly when the cover is perforated and used for lighting purposes, affixed by cords to the ceiling. But with soup-tureens it must be admitted that we have a wide latitude of choice, for they are round, oval, square and oblong; they may be ancestral or they may be Chinese, of faïence or of porcelain. And they are still in fashion!

CHAPTER VI

CARLSBAD

THE FIRST TIME I HAD HEARD THE WORD "SPA" AT SARA-
toga, I thought it was an abbreviation for "Springs"
but I could not understand why it should be written
with an "a" instead of an "r." When I was old enough
to go with my father to Carlsbad, where he took the
cure, I realized that although Saratoga might be the
"Queen of Spas" in America, she had her rivals abroad.
I was to see that however fashionable it might be considered to "take a cure" it was not held to be—as with
us—an occasion for the display of great wealth. Saratoga meant fashion *and* cure—Carlsbad, although it
was the chosen cure of European aristocracy, meant
cure *and* fashion, to mention one of the many gay ones
in Europe.

The informality of Carlsbad was borne in upon us
at the moment of our arrival, for as the carriage with
my father, my sister, and myself approached the hotel
entrance, we saw many of the guests rising from their
tables—not to salute us, but to step aside as the table
itself was grabbed so that the horses would not upset it
—for when tea was served, it was served in front of the
hotel and the tables were scattered over the roadway

with charming disregard of danger.

Having, as it were, ridden in on the tea-tables, my surprise was not great when I found that we walked out for breakfast, stopping first to see our father "take the waters" and then at Hamml's for bread which we carried along with us in pink paper bags—the pink bag being a sign that you had paid. For the bread was not popped into it from the wire-basket into which you had, yourself, put the pieces of zwieback until you paid. We breakfasted out of doors at the Freundschaftsalle or the more fashionable Kaiserspark.

There was a delightful and ridiculous little river, with bridges crossing it to the road; there were beautiful trees, and innumerable walks, which we took on the sterner days when my father did as he was told. Any morning when he said: "Let's unbend today," we knew we would be driving out and eating whatever we wanted to—and what *he* had probably been forbidden to eat.

Pierpont Morgan was there and had an ingenious way of seeing to it that the two eggs allowed him for his daily breakfast were as big as possible. He wore a ring on a chain; if the egg offered him could slip through it he refused that egg and called for another.

Colonel Jay, another Carlsbad guest, felt that he had mastered German when he could say—and say it he did with pride . . . "Morgen . . . Gehts. . . ." (Morgan —Gates his Wall Street friends.)

Instead of the familiar names of the Saratoga waters we mastered the new vocabulary of "Sprudel"—the

THE AUTHOR, AGED 9 AT DRESDEN

most popular, "Heilbrunnen" and "Schlossbrunnen";
my sister and I did not drink them except occasionally
but we accompanied my father to his spring.

Those were the days when spas were visited because
it was absolutely necessary to call a halt in the ordinary
régime. Mr. Morgan, Colonel Jay and the others, like
my father, had spent the year eating what they wanted
to, attending banquets on state occasions, and drinking,
not to excess, but enough to bring on rheumatism.
When that reached a really painful stage, the doctor
was sent for. His advice was followed for three weeks,
a month, six weeks, until the unpleasant symptoms
disappeared and one was "cured."

Whereupon, roast beef and Château Laffitte appeared on the menu again, without being questioned.
"Prevention" had no meaning. But "cure" had. Carlsbad served the doctors' purpose very well since it neces-
sitated an ocean voyage, in itself a rest for the business
man who could not find any at all when letters or tele-
grams reached him too easily. The radio, the trans-
Atlantic telephone had not yet arrived to disturb these
summer "cures."

Our voyage on the "Elbe" must have been one of
the first ones lighted by electricity, for I recall that the
steward would come into the "Ladies' Lounge," osten-
tatiously dust the glass bulbs when the light was on,
and then—if he could catch anyone's eye—nod signifi-
cantly and shake his head as much as to say: "The
miracle of progress which permits dusting lighted
lamps!"

CHAPTER VII

NEWPORT: THE PAGEANT

WHENEVER TODAY I LOOK THROUGH "THE HISTORY OF Chivalry"—for it is always on my table—I feel something of the same emotion that I did when my father gave it to me. It was one of the first books I ever owned. It was in color. The costumes enthralled me; they were gorgeous and they *meant* something. Even the trappings of the horses meant something, and the people who saw these knights coming towards them could read the devices.

My first idea of human personality really came from this book; it was external personality. You did not see the face of the knight in armor. You saw his crest, his arms, his device. I had the ingenuous notion that each knight made his own choice of these things; I never thought of his being born to the waving plumes, lances and shields, of his having to win his spurs. I was exceedingly vague about the feudal, but the glory of tournaments was over my childhood from the day I first possessed this book. Ceremonial became my ideal! Pageantry my dream!

"All they have to do is to beat the iron pot and light a light, and you'll be there!" Harry Lehr used to say mockingly.

Newport was certainly created for pageantry; and it is for that reason that it holds first place in my memory. There could have been no more perfect setting for the life which went on there every summer from the fourth of July until the end of the Horse Show in September. Absurd as it may seem, the colored postcards, at which we all used to rail, are not much too garish to give a vivid idea of the place.

It may be that the sand of Bailey's Beach was not quite so golden as that pictured in the "souvenir folder," nor the blue slates and red tiles of the roofs quite so brilliant, but there could be no exaggeration of the blue of the sky or of the soft cumulus clouds scattered between the horizon and the zenith. And nothing could be whiter than the marble, redder than the bricks, or greener than the lawns and the box-hedges, against which the stone-posts of the great gateways were so sharply outlined.

The first time I saw Newport my eyes were completely filled with its beauty; the air was so stimulating. New York seemed suddenly a dingy place full of unnecessary obstacles, useless formalities and disconcerting pauses. At Newport you were released from all formalities except those of this delightful pageant which continued, day after day, from the moment we waked up in brilliant sunshine to the moment we reluctantly left the lustre of moonlit or starlit night to go to bed. I was never tired.

It was not just the eye which was pleased. I remember so well the sound of the waves on the beach, the sound of the winds in a storm, but these may be heard in many other places. It was the sound of insects in the lovely sunken gardens of "Wakehurst," and the sound of fountains which seemed to me the music to which the pageant was set.

And there was such variety! Each of the great houses had its own background to offer for the parties given in it; no two of the terraces gave the same view of the stretch of water before them; farther inland, the other houses offered more intimate settings. We never felt we were moving in circles, seeing the same people, day after day; they seemed to change as we moved on and on towards the end of the season.

Then there was the picturesque old town itself with traditions which we all came to be proud of, even though we, the newcomers, were "intruders" to the older inhabitants. Newport had always considered itself distinguished because of the famous people who had lived there—Revolutionary heroes like Rochambeau and de Ternay, and later, General Prescott, Gilbert Stuart, whose house was still pointed out, and Lord Calvert, Charlotte Cushman and Julia Ward Howe.

The fabled old Mill belonged to more mysterious times, to that of the Vikings, perhaps. And if that were true, the skeleton in armor which had been found there in the early part of the last century must have belonged

THE STATE HOUSE, BROADWAY, NEWPORT

THE STONE TOWER, NEWPORT

Photographs by Brown Brothers

to some adventurous Norseman to whom Longfellow addressed the lines:

> "Speak, speak! Thou fearful guest!
> Who, with thy hollow breast,
> Still in rude armor drest,
> Comest to haunt me!"

How many times my mother had recited this poem to us; it had been written when the town was known best as a charming place for those ship-owning men who loved to stand on the open balcony or platform atop their houses to watch their ships come into the harbor.

The houses went down to the sea in terraces, like seats at a theater, and so each "Captain's walk," as the platform was called, had an unobstructed view. Little did these old houses dream of the change which the building of the great ones would bring about; nor did they ever seem to me to be much concerned with these changes; they were there in the old town—and there they are today.

The first outsiders to choose Newport for the summer were some families of the Old South who came up for the fine air; they were content to spend their vacation in small boarding-houses. When, however, Newport was discovered by visitors from Boston and New York, the famous old Ocean House came into existence.

It had just burned down, for the second and last

time, when we arrived at Newport, so that I never saw it. But it was associated with the days when music began at eleven o'clock in the morning and dinners were over long before nine, and when everybody, except on rare occasions, was in bed by eleven o'clock.

The delightful invention known as a "hop" did not come into the life of Newport until after the War of the Secession. Yet, even that innovation allowed the gayest of the gay to be in bed before midnight. It sounded like a Kate Greenaway era, sandwiched in between the more formal Colonial period and our own which stands out in the history of the town as the one when tradesmen were in despair if certain members of the Newport "Colony" were absent because, as the papers said: "five hundred thousand dollars less will be spent this year."

In those early days when everyone went out for a drive it was always along the roads which led deeper into the island. For that reason the real estate venture of Governor Lawrence looked like madness to the residents. He bought the windy and treeless Ochre Point tract and cut it up into building lots and sold them. He made a fortune. To the Islanders, who much preferred their own tidy little homes, the palatial houses which went up, one after the other, seemed out of another world. They were indeed.

But the greatest change to come over the place was when one of the summer colony decided that he would live at Newport as they were living in the fashionable centers of Europe. He put his servants into livery! The natives stared; this set the pace for all the other great houses.

Liveried servants of course were English and "used to the harness." Formality was very visible in Bellevue Avenue, "with its mêlée of expensive cars and their expensive owners,"—as Freddy Martin wrote so condescendingly. He considered it as "artificial as the unnatural-looking clumps of blue hydrangeas, Newport's favorite flower." He preferred the days of "rose-covered cottages." Yet, even in those days, Ward McAllister had written: "This Newport is no place for a man without a fortune." Most unfortunately for him, and his hope of making a fortune, he had bought his farm on the wrong side of town—the north side which never became fashionable.

It must be admitted that there was nothing very homelike or cozy about the look of the new palaces as they loomed against the sky, even though trees had been set out all about them. One evening at the Clambake Club, a visiting Englishman pointed out the huge square structure of the Cornelius Vanderbilt home and asked me what it was.

"That is the Breakers," I said, as one would say: "That is the Château of Versailles," or "Westminster."

"Ah, the Breakers," he repeated. "I *knew* it must be a hotel."

The first serious dissension between those who called Newport their home and those who called it their "playground" started when the owners of the great houses began to sink the "cliff-walk" so that strolling promenaders could not look in on their grounds. Everyone, by law, had the right to walk on the edge of the cliffs, and since that right could not be taken from them there was nothing to do but to cut the walk down so that those who passed along it in the exercise of their rights could not, however, gaze upon the owners of the properties and their guests.

What the leaders in the houses, which now were scattered thickly over this side of the island, could not prevent was the curiosity of the society reporters who had come to look at Newport as the greatest of the summer hunting grounds. They fixed their hungry gaze upon all the gaiety and fashion, exaggerated its importance for the sake of increasing their own and aroused an interest in the doings of the Newport colony such as had never before been awakened by any circle of merry-makers.

Newport at last was Newport—the American capital of luxury and extravagance. All of us who spent our summers there now, had to reconcile ourselves to playing in the limelight. Not that much reconciliation was necessary. We read the reports of our doings much more eagerly I suppose than anyone else, for they gave us a sort of perspective upon our circle, converting it very often into a series of triangles, whose story sounded like rather malicious gossip but might have some truth in it!

Brown Brothers, photo.

'THE BREAKERS,' CORNELIUS VANDERBILT'S NEWPORT RESIDENCE

Now owned by Count and Countes László Szechenyi

Then there were the books which appeared from time to time written by foreign guests as well as others who had spent a day or a week with us but who invariably gave us at least a chapter. For, no matter how supercilious the guest might wish to appear in writing his memoirs he knew, and we knew, that his success or failure at Newport was the final social test of his American tour. He might want, in retrospect, to show his scorn for the untitled American but he knew that had he not been invited to the houses of these untitled ones he would have been very much mortified. He might not even have troubled to write his memoirs had he not been able to boast of this hospitality in the richest and most discussed summer colony in the world.

When the Marquis de Castellane wrote his "Confessions" he devoted his chapter to us which sounded like sincere appreciation until you ran on this:

"Everyone at Newport was most kind and hospitable. And a succession of dinners, fêtes and picnics were given in my honor. I have rarely met more hospitable people than Americans when *they have a motive for hospitality.*"

The italics are mine. Our motive in his case—if there had to be one to explain our invitations—was to have his wit and dainty manners grace our parties; he amused us because he was so unlike other guests we had had,—very unlike those of more imposing title and position. Dainty he must have recognized himself to be for he wrote: "I was not, however, intrigued by the cuisine, with its terrapin, its clam broth, its oyster crabs; neither was I overwhelmed by the methods of entertaining. If spending money to excess constitutes a claim to success, many Americans can lay claim to it."

He might not have liked our "methods of entertaining" but where did he get terrapin at Newport in summer? Clam broth and oyster crabs, yes. We all liked them and whenever we went off for the day and lunched in the open air they were our choice. Indeed, one of the nice things about Newport was that you could eat mussels if you wished without apologizing because they were not a costly dish.

Not so at Great South Bay—my mother, who was inordinately fond of them, used to suffer in her pride whenever she ordered them there. From the air of the head-waiter she perceived that she had fallen in his estimation, since mussels only cost about two or three cents a pound. She would confide to him that she had ordered them, not because she liked them but because the doctor had recommended them as part of her diet. But very often even this subterfuge failed to re-establish her sense of self-esteem and she would not be able to enjoy the dish when it had been set, with an air of great condescension, before her.

At Newport mussels were accepted without condescension. At one luncheon a visiting Englishman took the proffered dish of mussels from the hand of the footman and calmly dumped all its contents upon his

Brown Brothers, photo

MRS. CORNELIUS VANDERBILT

plate, saying with the utmost good humor: "I have eaten these before and found them very good, really very good!"

So had we, but there we sat with empty plates, for no other mussels had been prepared in the kitchen. We watched him enjoy himself. It was a pleasant sight. The hostess was the only one who looked daggers at him. But as his eyes were upon his plate he missed that.

Harry Lehr once did the same thing with asparagus, of which he was very fond, but *he* did it with malice aforethought and enjoyed the consternation of the four other guests when they saw that he had taken it all. This time his hostess was the only one who stayed serene; she leaned over: "Your telephone number, my dear Harry?"

He looked puzzled, he knew that she knew it; but he answered: "One, eight, four, three."

"On the present occasion, one eight *for six*," she replied.

Beginning with the fourth of July, we kept up the pace at Newport until the end of the Horse Show— Saturday evening of the first week in September. The days were filled with yachting, luncheons, dinners or excursions of some sort. And when I think how many times a week during the season at Newport the same ones of us met together, it speaks well for our dispositions that we were so seldom bored, that there were so

few misunderstandings, and that we did not die of indi-
gestion . . . yet. . . .

"You don't give parties to enjoy yourselves," said
Jimmy Cutting, "but to advance yourselves."

And I suppose it was this competition among us
which kept up the interest. The cooks must have been
driven to it to find striking novelties for the frequent
dinners. Not long ago I came across an "agenda" of
mine in which I had written down all the dinners of
one season; the list, at first glance, gives nothing but
the names of the hosts and the hour—usually half past
eight, occasionally eight o'clock, but with the names of
the houses themselves added, the picture of Newport
emerges as lovely as ever.

The ball was that year set rolling by Mrs. Reginald
Vanderbilt who gave a dinner on Sunday, the third of
July, at "Sandy Point Farms," that old-fashioned farmhouse which had been delightfully remodelled and enlarged some five years before. The low ceilings and
dark woodwork, the cretonnes and the homelike fur-
nishings put this among the most charming of the old
places at Newport.

Reginald Vanderbilt had had a racing track laid
out with boxes for us to sit in and watch his horses
being trained, a stand in the middle for the brass band
which enlivened the scene. I remember an odd mirror
set in a horse-collar and, underneath, a silver plaque
with the name of the horse and the dates of its
triumphs; Reggie also had the first complete bar ever

installed in a private mansion.

Yet, according to Cornelius Vanderbilt, Junior, Reggie's nephew, no such new enterprise should have been possible, for that young man writes in his "Farewell to Fifth Avenue" that when McKinley was assassinated in September, 1901, "the party was over. So was the America of Newport Masqueraders. . . . They felt, these bearers of America's greatest names, that from then on they would have to run as fast as they could in order to remain in place, so that the nightmare of the future might not become the terror of the present."

The news of the assassination had stunned us, as it stunned the whole country. No big parties were given for the rest of the season; we all wore black until after the funeral. But I do not recall any terrifying predictions and, had they been made, I would have heard them, for this was my first season in Newport and everything that was said and done there interested me and engraved itself on my memory.

Here we were, nine years after "the party was over," having dinner with the Vanderbilts and if there was any running it would be done by the blood horses whose career we would follow up to their appearance at the Horse Show.

It is very easy to be a retrospective prophet.

On Monday, the fourth of July, we dined at Mrs. Herman Oelrichs' "Rosecliff," one of the most beautiful places of Newport. There is no hint on my day-book as to what the entertainment was that night; it may be that it was nothing but a dinner, but in that case it would be a perfect dinner, without a flaw, for Tessie Oelrichs had a passion for perfection. She never did anything by halves. When she had a full circus out from New York, with side-shows and peanuts, not only did the guests have a rarely good time, the performers themselves were shown all sorts of attentions and went back enchanted with a profitable and perfect day's outing and for dummies she illuminated her grounds and even the ocean itself.

We never arrived at Newport at our hired houses that we did not find the beds all made up with fresh linen, towels on the racks, lamp-shades . . . everything, even to fresh fruit waiting for us, before the servants could have had a chance to do what was needed for our comfort. With a note wishing us welcome were the latest magazines and papers. She had thought out all the details of the arrival and taken away any trace of discomfort or bleakness—and that without telling us that she would do it.

All her friends came to depend upon her when there was need of something being done in haste. When one of them brought his dying wife back from Europe, where he had taken her in hope that certain doctors could help her, it was Tessie Oelrichs who had the responsibility of renting a house for them at Newport, and seeing to all those details which are so important when anyone is ill, linen and silver, screens in the sick-

Brown Brothers, photo

MRS. HERMAN OELRICHS

room, extra service for the nurses.

But when the wife died, in spite of all the devotion lavished upon her, we were more than amazed at the way her two daughters behaved after the funeral. They asked their stepfather if they could go to the New York house which he had built just before deciding to go to Europe for consultation and where he had given just one big dinner before sailing.

"We want so much to get a few souvenirs of our mother," they said. And the grief-stricken widower told them to go and take what they wanted.

Some time later, with Mrs. Oelrichs to keep him company, he faced the tragedy of going back to New York to visit the house which he had hoped would be his home.

It had been literally denuded! Those young women had not only taken all the little things which might have belonged to their mother but they had taken the fine panelled woodwork, the bathtubs and basins, the very flooring itself, so that you had to be careful where you stepped!

After the first shock, their step-father said sadly: "I could never have lived here again anyway. Fix it up, Tessie, and we'll sell it."

"A few souvenirs!" said Mrs. Oelrichs. "I'm glad they left the walls!" and she ordered in the workmen.

Yet, perhaps, it was this very talent for doing things perfectly which had brought about the separation of the Oelrichs; she was a born manager and a man might

resent that ability of hers. She, herself, was so aware
of her passion for order and cleanliness that she used to
say:

"When I die, bury me with a cake of sapolio in one
hand and a scrubbing-brush in the other; they are my
symbols."

Indeed, I have seen her go down on her knees when
a servant insisted that a marble floor could not be any
cleaner than she had made it and, taking the brush
from the girl's hand, prove the contrary.

She had her beds made up fresh every day, would
never sleep in sheets which did not belong to her, so
that even at the Ritz here in Paris her own bed—which
was kept between-times at the Maison de Blanc—was
set up the day before she arrived and taken down the
day after she left, which meant that she always paid for
those two extra days.

Whenever she left New York for Newport, or "Rosecliff" for New York, her house was in perfect order,
everything closed except her bedroom: that she left as
though she were going to sleep there that same night
—no slip-covers on the furniture, the bed made up—
she was superstitious about it.

"If I didn't know that I could come in at any moment and find everything ready for me, it would feel
like death," she'd say.

Yet she demanded little attention from a maid,
would not have a personal maid, for she could not bear
to have anyone touch her hair or herself, or be stand-

ing around holding a garment for her. On her dressing-table there was always a large glass bowl of water which she used in doing her hair, that beautiful hair that had a delightful tendency to curl. Whatever was to be mended or arranged would have a paper with directions pinned to it. Every morning the maid came in only for these.

Her aloofness made her seem indifferent to her beauty—for she was beautiful; she would never let anyone paint her portrait; she did not even want to have photographs taken, and it was a triumph to get her to join in a group, or with me, so that we could have a picture of her.

Undoubtedly her deafness was responsible for this self-chosen isolation; it may have meant a condition of nerves which we others could not guess. But she never spoke of it. She listened very intently so as not to tire you more than could be helped when you talked with her. And she herself spoke much too loud and in an unmodulated voice which used to give us some anxiety when we were out in the world with her.

One day at Monte Carlo we were in the dining-room of the Sporting Club at luncheon with a third woman; the only other person in the room was a good-looking man at a table in the corner, to whom we paid no heed.

"I see that Beatrice has married her third," said Mrs. Oelrichs. "I wonder how long it will last," and, turning to me, "How long do you think she will stand this one, Bessie?"

I don't remember what I answered, but she went on talking of the other two husbands and their qualities which had it seemed exasperated Beatrice, even though she had had a child each time and seemed quite happy. We listened much amused while she put on all the embroidery to the story of a spoiled girl and her two divorces.

Just as she came to the end of her tale, which could have been distinctly heard in the corners of a much larger room, in came Beatrice herself and joined the man at the near table!

The silence which fell upon us was not broken until Beatrice, all smiles, brought over the gentleman . . . "I want you to meet my new husband," she said.

Mrs. Oelrichs lived all alone in her big houses when she was not entertaining house-guests. And she did not know what fear was. At night, after she had been out to a dinner or the opera in New York, she would let herself in with her latchkey, take the lift and go up past the dark drawing-room floor to her own room without the slightest anxiety; she did not keep the servants up for her return. That was part of her thoughtfulness—or her love of independence, whichever way you preferred to take it.

I was with her that evening when, after the San Francisco earthquake, she was waiting in New York for her husband to come back from San Francisco— they had been living apart for several years—but she was still in love with him.

At the first news of the disaster she had telegraphed for someone to open the family vault out at the cemetery; she knew what even that sort of a shelter would mean to those who were without any other. Then she had gone down to Brooks Brothers and bought a complete outfit for Herman Oelrichs, knowing that he must have lost everything. She ordered every sort of suit he could possibly need, all the underwear and dressing-gowns, cravats and shoes—she was in a state of happy excitement, she had his rooms freshened up, new toilet articles laid out. The house was filled with flowers, the dinner was ordered—for she knew the train by which he would be arriving. They would dine alone but I was staying there until he came.

As the hour passed in which he should have appeared, had he come from the station, she grew more and more rigid and white—*could* not listen—since she heard almost nothing, so she kept her eyes, first on the clock and then on the door. It opened finally—but it was not her husband, it was Herbert, the butler, who came in to tell her that Mr. Oelrichs had gone directly to his club. He had seen him walking up Fifth Avenue.

CHAPTER VIII

THE YACHT

ON TUESDAY OF THAT FIRST WEEK AT NEWPORT, WE
dined on the *"May,"* the yacht which belonged to my
cousin, Mrs. Van Rensselaer, who was a Drexel and
one of the only two women ever to be made "Captain"
by the Philadelphia Yacht Club, if I remember rightly.

Yachts were an extension of Newport; they added to
the Arabian Nights' atmosphere which hovered over
the place during the long days and the short nights
of the season there. "Pleasure yachts" they were called
at first, and then the word "pleasure" was dropped
since the yacht itself had come to symbolize pleasure,
and the moment it was used for anything else, any com-
mercial end, it ceased to be a "yacht."

Some of them came into Newport from distant ports
to anchor for only a few days; some few had the added
glory of having encircled the globe; all of them remained part of the year out of commission, as their
owners were business men. All of them were beautiful
as they lay at anchor in sunlight or moonlight.

Their names were considered of the greatest importance. *May* was most unusually simple. The *Nour-
mahal* (Light of the Harem) which belonged to John

Jacob Astor was the sort of name which appealed. The *Sultana* belonged to John R. Drexel, my cousin, and, commuting between New York and Newport, had a full corps of servants, with a famous chef at their head, who did not disembark at either end any more than the crew did.

Grace Vanderbilt was asking suggestions one day for a suitable name for a racing yacht—beginning with a "V"—when a man who was there made a most impudent one: *Vandal*. They called it finally, the *Vanitie*.

Mr. Leeds had no difficulty in finding a name for his yacht; he called it the *Noma* from the first letters of Mrs. Leeds' maiden name, Nonnie May.

"It is a good name to send through the megaphone," Mr. Leeds would say, putting his hands suddenly to his mouth and shouting to prove it.

On this yacht everything had to be unusual: lights must not be just lights—they must suggest the sea, so they were behind crystal turtle-shells, held to the wall by their bronze feet and head. The salt and pepper-shakers were tiny terrestrial globes.

On Eugene Higgins' *Varuna*, the ash-trays were miniature life-boats—not a bad reminder of the risk of fire from a cigarette. A ship's captain once told me that cigarettes were the greatest danger which menaced a ship at sea.

Everything on the *Varuna* was done in the most perfect maritime style. Eugene Higgins spent so much time on it that he had a gymnasium fitted out for himself, kept a fencing master on board with whom he practised every day, to keep fit, and delighted his guests by presenting them with souvenirs when they left the yacht—one of which I still have: a scarf-pin of two crossed flags—the one belonging to the New York Yacht Club, the other white with two crescents of blue, joined together, which made an "H." He used to send the hostesses of Newport his yacht done as a flower piece—of small blossoms.

Another yacht with an Oriental name was my uncle's, Anthony Drexel's *Semiramis*. After his death it was sold to Harry Walters, Commodore of the New York Yacht Club. That was the *Narada*—for he changed the name. We looked forward to its arrival at Newport because of the fairy-like entertainments he gave on it— brilliant and costly. For everything connected with a yacht is expensive. I once heard a man say to Mr. Astor:

"I think I'll have a yacht next year. How much does it cost?"

"The minute you ask how much it costs," replied Mr. Astor, "you might just as well drop the idea."

Coming back to the day-book, I find that the four remaining dinners of that first week of the season were one which we gave on Wednesday, the one at "Fairholme" of the John R. Drexel's, the ones given on Friday by Mrs. Whitney Warren and on Saturday by Mrs. George McFadden.

The next week we gave two dinners, one large, prob-

NEWPORT HARBOR

YACHTS ROUNDING BRENTON REEF LIGHTSHIP

Photographs by Brown Brothers

ably forty or sixty, and the other small; we spent two days on the *Sultana* going to the wedding of Mrs. Stuyvesant Fish's son at Garrison-on-the-Hudson. And the other three nights were spent at dinners with Mrs. Cornelius Vanderbilt, Mrs. James Lanier and Mr. Van Alen, Mrs. Astor's son-in-law, whose daughters helped him entertain because he was a widower.

And a widower so much sought after that he made a delightful pretence of being afraid on the one hand that he would be caught, or sometimes on the other, that his popularity with the ladies might wane—those ladies being for the most party marriageable widows— and seldom absent from his mind. One winter, in Mrs. Astor's box at the Opera he fell asleep in the shadow at the back of it. He wakened with a start.

"Was I asleep?" he asked, anxiously.

"You certainly were," I replied.

"Was I snoring?"

"You were not."

His face beamed—"Spread that around among the widows, won't you?" he said.

The third week saw us at only four formal dinners, one of them at Mrs. Oelrichs', another at Lispenard Stewart's "White Lodge"—a perfectly kept old bachelor's mansion where he gave dinners in a room beautifully decorated by Walter Crane. But no balls, though he had a large and well-appointed ballroom—we always thought he considered them too destructive of his tranquil surroundings.

There were doubtless as many luncheons as dinners since the weather at Newport did not get too hot until late in August for us to enjoy midday entertainments, particularly as we all met on the Beach in the morning,—Bailey's Beach which Cornelius Vanderbilt, Junior, has expressed such contempt for when it seems to me that it could not have been better kept by those beach-men, dressed in white, who worked there in the mornings. He must have seen it only in recent years, for in our time it was so gay, with rows of bath-houses with initials painted upon them to show to whom they belonged. It was here that tennis was played for the first time—on an exquisite green lawn close to the beach—in bathing suits! A far cry from the tennis costumes of Saratoga!

Just as at New York, Mrs. Astor's dinners were one of the big events of the season. In the year of which I am writing, one was given on the night of August second. The next night Mr. Van Alen gave another dinner at "Wakehurst," and the night following Mrs. Elisha Dyer gave her second dinner of the season at "Wayside"—that house of yellow brick which—being superstitious about living in a new house—they had made over for their entertaining. Mrs. Dyer never forgave Tessie Oelrichs' stopping in front of it one day and saying to someone with her, in a voice which reached the owner, invisible in the garden, . . .

"There it is: a Queen Anne front and a Mary Anne back!"

On the Friday of this week, my cousin, Mrs. Craig Biddle, gave her dinner at "Nethercliff" and we gave ours at "Arleigh," where we could, if we wished, have a hundred and fifty guests without being crowded.

And so it went on, with dinners and dinner-dances until, as always, Mrs. Fish would give her farewell dinner and ball on the last night of the Horse Show. When "Home, Sweet Home" was played as a sign that the ball was over, we all separated and scattered to White Sulphur Springs, to Long Island, or to homes along the Hudson to "rest up" for the New York season.

At one of Mrs. Fish's parties when "Home, Sweet Home" was being played, I recall seeing an Englishman who, observing the general movement of the guests, rose and stood at attention; he thought he was hearing the national anthem!

One evening an enthusiastic dancer came up to Mamie and begged that in spite of the closing music there might be one more two-step.

"Just one more two-step," she pleaded.

"There are just two more steps for you," said Mrs. Fish. "One upstairs to get your wraps, the other out to your carriage."

But since there was no malice in what Mrs. Fish said,

she was like a bit of fresh air in any group. You never knew what she was going to say and she usually said it. She could not stand the banal question, asked for the mere sake of keeping up conversation. A man we knew who had been away for several years from Garrison and, now that he was back, was trying to make up for his absence by renewed interest, observed the new bridge and asked with enthusiasm:

"Well, how did *that* get here?"

"That bridge?" said Mamie. "Why, I had it, and it was most painful!"

Nor was Mr. Fish behind her in the way of repartee when he was at all interested in a conversation. Someone was talking about one of their friends whose family increased every year. Turning to Mr. Fish, she asked: "Have you seen Mrs. N's last baby?"

"No, I haven't," he replied seriously. "I don't expect to live that long."

Mr. Fish did not care for Newport, spent very little time there, and did not like to have his sons stay there more than a few days each season. So Glenclyffe Farms, the fine old family place on the Hudson, across from West Point, was kept open all the year round. But Mamie could not stay anywhere without company. And fortunately two of her friends could be counted upon to come at a moment's notice; she would ring one or the other up in New York and out she would come for as long as required.

One day at Newport we arrived to take lunch with

Mrs. Fish and found all the fifty guests assembled but no hostess in sight. At last I went upstairs and found her sitting dejectedly in front of her dressing-table:

"I wish those people would go away!" she said as I came in. "I don't want them. Why can't they go home?"

"But you invited them yourself four weeks ago," I said.

"Four weeks ago I thought I wanted them to come, but I have changed my mind."

She finally consented to go down.

Another time she came in to greet her guests gathered for dinner.

"Make yourselves perfectly at home," she said laughingly. "And believe me! There is no one wishes you there more heartily than I do."

Which was not unlike her response to an embarrassed guest who had to leave a musicale she was giving before it was over.

"I promised my sister that I would call for her . . ."

"Don't apologize," broke in Mamie, "and remember, no guest ever left too soon for me!"

"I'm so tired of being hypocritically polite," she complained one evening when we had arrived, the first of the guests invited for dinner. There was something in the way she said it which made it a declaration of importance, and we were not surprised to see her greet the next person who came in, somewhat red in the face and agitated, with: "You certainly look flustered,

Mr. So-and-so."

Then to a woman who had suffered as we all did in the windy porte-cochère of the "Crossways": "You look rather wind-tossed, Mrs. B." But, most disconcerting of all, to a third—"Oh, how do you do, Mr. S.! I had quite forgotten I asked you."

Another time she electrified her dinner guests at the beginning of a new season by saying: "Well, here you all are, older faces and younger clothes."

Perhaps one reason I felt so comfortable when I was with Mrs. Fish was that she did not pretend to care any more for music than I did. When someone asked her what instrument she played, she said very seriously: "A comb."

Above all she disliked listening to musicians after a dinner or at a musicale.

"I'm never sure that I have fixed my face right," she used to say, "for sometimes when it is just right for expressing appreciation of a cradle song, I find I'm listening to the 'Cry of the Valkyries'; or when I've fixed it for the 'Two Grenadiers' they sing the duet from 'Romeo and Juliet.'"

She used to wear what she called her "seven-dollar curls"; they came off one day as she was entering Mrs. Gould's house. The liveried servant nearest to her picked them up and presented them to her with a low bow. She was still pinning them in place as she came

Brown Brothers, photo.

MRS. STUYVESANT FISH   MISS LOLA ROBINSON

into the room where we were.

"Sweet pet," she said to her hostess, "you must discharge your man; my secret is known to him."

"Which man was it?" asked Mrs. Gould, somewhat dismayed.

"I haven't the slightest idea," said Mamie, "all your men look exactly alike."

She did not save up her repartee for company either. One evening at Garrison's she had a fit of coughing which worried Mr. Fish who was standing on the verandah with her.

"Can I get something for your throat, my dear?" he asked.

"Yes, you can," she answered.

"Well, what?"

"That diamond and pearl necklace that I saw today at Tiffany's."

He laughed. But the next time I saw her she was wearing it.

One day we were asking each other in one of those infantile games what the favorite flower of each one was. Mrs. Fish had roused laughter by choosing the lily; then she turned to Harry Lehr:

"I know your favorite flower," she said. "It's the marigold."

CHAPTER IX

DOMESTIC CATASTROPHES

"THE WAY OF THE ENTERTAINER IS HARD!" THE OLD Duchess of Manchester used to say. And the truth of that complaint has been borne in upon me for many years. There is no way of insuring yourself against the catastrophes which a guest may introduce into your tranquil home. Until you have entertained a man or woman you cannot be sure whether they are not born under a destructive star, whether they do not—as appearances seem to indicate—belong to some secret society devoted to devastating interiors.

When you discover that star or that society, it is too late to prevent the consequences of their visit. I am not thinking merely of that pot of hot coffee which a guest spilled over a satin-covered comforter at Mrs. Belmont's, nor of the wet muff of dyed fur thrown carelessly upon a silk-embroidered bed-spread, from which the stain could never be taken, nor of the marks left by a heavy suit-case thumped upon the bed for the owner to pack at his ease.

I am thinking of that guest at "Beaulieu" who, taking two big vases off a mantel, climbed up and after a great deal of trouble opened a window above, which had never until then been opened, there being two others in that room. Then she replaced the vases. The maid, coming in a moment after, the draught from the door blew the window shut; as it shut, it swept those rare vases, clock and all, off the mantel; their crash was enough to make Mrs. Belmont in her study below jump to her feet.

But she did not rush upstairs; she waited for her guest to explain the noise when she came down to lunch.

Lunch was over and nothing had been explained— Mrs. Belmont asked:

"What was that fearful noise I heard in your room this morning?"

"Oh, did you hear it?" replied the guest sympathetically. "When the maid brought in my breakfast, the window slammed shut and knocked the things off the mantel. Wasn't it stupid of her!"

A cousin of mine was visiting me; his man-servant, carrying up his breakfast, stumbled. Over the bannister went the tray with a terrific crash. Servants rushed to the scene. Every piece of china was, as the poet would say, in shards. The silver tea-set itself was so battered it would have to be sent back to the shop to be rounded out again.

"Thomas ought not to drink before breakfast," said my cousin meditatively. "I must speak to him about it."

Sometimes the carelessness of a guest is expensive although the accident is slight. I saw one of mine talk-

ing animatedly to another, the lighted end of her cigarette against the velvet upholstery of one of my dining-
room chairs. I called her attention to it. Too late!
There was the neat round hole with a delicately singed
border.

It spoiled the set, since the velvet could not be
matched.

And in front of a fireplace there is the cigarette
burn in the white marble hearth-stone, signature of
the lady who missed the fire when she tossed the butt
of her cigarette negligently towards it. Such a burn as
that must be cut out of the marble and as the cut would
show as much as the stain why cut it?

There is more than one chapter to be written on
stains—and there are stains of all sorts—like those made
by transient visitors who come for tea and finding they
have sticky fingers from the cake-fillings, or from the
cream, wipe them—surreptitiously of course—on the
curtains of the window near which they are standing—
not the washable tulle curtains, but on the silk ones.

I know of one woman who was the guest of a friend
while continuing to take her treatments for reducing.
These included some liquid which she put in her bath:
when she left, the tub had to be taken out and another
put in because the reducing medicine had eaten all the
enamel from it. I suggested that a tub made out of the
stone which they used for laboratory tables might be
a practical idea when she came next.

And hair-tonic!

Another friend told me of a guest whose record I am sure has never been broken. He was, she said, a "charming fellow" in great demand as dinner guest and dancing partner and he was invited to spend a week with herself and her son. When he left, they discovered that the "charming fellow" had wiped off his razors on the embroidered part of the linen sheet but, worse than that, he had spilled a quart bottle of hair-tonic on a fine rug, ruining it and then running off on to the hardwood floor which was so discolored that it had to be taken up and replaced. His room was next to that of the son; the two men were the same size. When he left, his host had to outfit himself completely in shirts, collars and handkerchiefs. Only their taste in cravats, it seemed, differed: he had taken no cravats.

Ink makes the classic stain—yet, with care, it can be used by civilized beings without too great damage—certainly not such as that done by an Englishwoman, member of the nobility, who was visiting friends of mine; when she had gone they found that, liking to stay in bed to write her letters, she had used the linen sheets and the pale blue silk bed-curtains to wipe her pen on—not once, not accidentally, but with an evident meticulousness!

In a fine old castle in Holland where I was visiting a few years ago, the housekeeper came rushing down to our host in great dismay.

"Please come up and see the room which the Marquis of X. has left!" she said.

We had just said good-bye to the Marquis, sorry to have so delightful a guest leave before the rest of the house-party. But, once in his room, we understood the agitation of the housekeeper: it was perfectly evident that the beginning of the catastrophe had been the upsetting of a large inkwell which, half empty, was still on the table. The table was ruined and the large pink brocaded arm chair in front of it. To wipe table and chair, the guest had used a very large bath-towel and then had dragged it across the handsome rug, and what was even worse, over the lovely old rather absorbent tiles of his bathroom floor. Nothing could ever take out that stain: the tiles themselves would have to be changed!

And, on leaving, not a word either to the house-keeper or to his host!

It is hard for the entertainer to suit everyone:

"You have only two kinds of perfume in your coat-room," said a man to me recently, "and neither one of them is a scent I like."

I pointed out to a woman-guest one day that this same room had a rubberized floor, so that if anything dropped on it there was less chance of it breaking. The next time she came to my house she approached me rather aggressively:

"I dropped my vanity case on that floor of yours," she said, "just to see if it was rubber, and it was *marble!* I think you ought to buy me a new vanity case."

I felt distressed until she admitted that she had not made the experiment in the dressing-room but in the outer hall, where the floor *is* red and white marble. Yet in her mind I will always be the one at fault.

But, although that adventurous scientific experiment showed that the lady thought the marble was rubber-flooring, she was not like the man discovered by the Comte de Castellane as he was moistening his handkerchief with the tip of his tongue and then rubbing the reddish grain of a marble column in the hall to see if it were real or painted.

"I assure you," said the Comte approaching him politely, "it is no falser than your face."

It was a guest of Mrs. Fish's who was complaining to another as she came unexpectedly into the room: "There really were not enough bath-towels. I had to dry myself on the bath-mat."

"Indeed!" said Mamie, "You were lucky not to be offered the door-mat!"

Fortunate the host or hostess who has the gift of quick response and does not show his or her utter amazement—for the entertainer does hear odd bits of comment—as did Tessie Oelrichs, who had just given a musicale to inaugurate her new organ at Rosecliff, and thought her guests still under the spell of the music as they went off to the buffet. At least she thought so until taking up the telephone, she found someone was on the line; she recognized the voice of a man who had just left.

"There was really not enough food," she heard him saying, "no chicken salad . . . no lobster . . ."

Tessie broke in: "I am awfully sorry, Mr. X., but you see I was not giving a luncheon, I only invited you to a musicale."

But none of us ever suffered as much from entertaining as the French nobleman whose château in Auvergne was burned to the ground because her spirit lamp exploded when a week-end guest was heating her hair-curler. That "accident" was one of the most tragic I have ever known, for this château had been in his family for hundreds of years. It was filled with heirlooms; all the family portraits, all the family archives were in it. And not a thing was saved—not even the money on hand to pay the farmers and servants.

"I had to begin life all over again," he said when telling me of the disaster.

"But your guest?" I asked. "What did she do?"

"She was really very sorry," he replied.

But no matter how hard the path of entertaining might seem, we kept on doing it at Newport; once in a while someone would rebel. Mrs. Fish complained one day that she was tired of it.

"Why don't you take a moor in Scotland?" asked Jimmie Cutting. "Then we'll come over and shoot."

"Why don't I?" replied Mrs. Fish. "Because I would like to be a guest myself sometimes."

Yet it was Mrs. Fish who had the most original ideas for entertaining and kept Newport on its tiptoes, as when she was able, in some mysterious way, to get Jimmie Cutting to give a party himself—for while he lived on a little farm which he rented in the summer he was not given to inviting anyone out there to see him.

I suppose Mamie must have put it to him point blank that we were all wondering why he was so inhospitable, for she never hesitated to tell him what she thought, as on that occasion when he said he was going to spend two weeks at So-and-So's house. . . .

"And that is all that you *will* spend," she said.

At any rate he told her to invite whom she wished and he would have dinner ready. She said there would be eight. We were there in front of his little farmhouse in good time.

"Bring a lantern, Jimmie," Mamie called, as the carriage stopped. "Some of your guests cannot walk."

His state of mind on hearing that can be imagined. He brought the lantern and watched Mrs. Fish and Harry assist a life-sized mannequin to the dining-room. She was dressed as a bride, white shoes and stockings on her useless feet, white gloves on her helpless hands, and on her bosom a large locket from the five and ten cent store, with the initial of a certain lady dear to the heart of Jimmie, to whom he had been paying court for some time—ineffectual court, perhaps.

The other four guests included Mrs. Fish's two dogs,

one parrot and a framed copy of a portrait of a Spanish Infanta!

It was at Easton's Beach that Mrs. Belmont gave a party which caused a sensation by its simplicity. Easton's Beach was public; its very lack of exclusiveness was in its favor with Mrs. Belmont who had already embarked upon her campaign for women's votes. She engaged the whole beach with all the "attractions" for the evening, paying the equivalent of the usual gate receipts as well as all the expenses.

In making out her list, she had told her secretary to leave out certain names. But do not imagine that for an instant decorum kept the excluded ones silent when they realized they were not asked. As soon as the invitations were out recriminations began. I was with her one morning when we met one of the uninvited who began in her Southern drawl:

"Ah-h, Miss Alva, you were the first friend we had here at Newport, and you haven't invited us to your Saturday party."

"No, I haven't," said Mrs. Belmont, true to form.

"But we are so fond of you, Miss Alva."

"I'm not doubting your affection," replied Mrs. Belmont, "but I've seen the lights in your windows every Saturday evening and you have never invited my young guest Inez Milholland to *your* parties. Not even after I told you she danced."

"Well," said the disappointed one, "we'll have to

Brown Brothers, photo.

MRS. OLIVER H. P. BELMONT

make a hole in the wall and peek in."

"Oh?" said Mrs. Belmont. "I certainly hope for your sake that it doesn't rain."

Off we went to meet "by chance" one or another of the excluded Newportites, none of whom made any pretence of not being hurt; each one begging to know why he or she was being so harshly treated. And they all found out, but that did not mean that they were invited.

Mrs. Fish sometimes went in for simplicity, too; and on one occasion she gave a picnic at which we did all the serving. At another one we would have been as well pleased if again there had been no servants, for when the hour came for lunch and we were waiting with lively appetites, acquired by a morning of unwonted exercise, we found that the footmen, seized no doubt by a sudden carelessness induced by too many mid-morning drinks, had eaten it all up! There was nothing for us to do but to go home hungry—one of those occasions where the dispositions of guests may be studied to advantage.

But picnics, whether on the beach or deeper within the island, were likely to be spontaneous affairs, depending upon the weather. The season's real program was more fixed; the dinners and especially the balls had to be arranged as far beforehand as possible. There was the "Number One" group of hostesses who used to get to Newport early, meet at one of our houses and decide upon the events of the season. This was in order that dinners and balls should not interfere with each other.

There was a group "Number Two" whose parties did occasionally interfere with ours when they had had the good fortune to have their invitations accepted by some visiting personages, native or foreign. I heard a Number One matron exclaim one night as she wiped from an ashes-of-roses gown the jelly which the butler had dropped on it: "I shall never accept a Number Two invitation again!"

All of us had preferences for certain days of the week and no one wanted Monday. "Blue Monday" is not an empty phrase at a resort where all the detached and useful young men, and many of the hosts, have left on Sunday night after dinner for New York or Philadelphia.

It was for that reason that we appreciated the constant presence, during the season, of certain young men, usually diplomats, who could afford a long vacation and could be counted upon even for Monday affairs.

One of the most popular of this number was a man I'll call Donald Grayson.

He was a tall, red-haired, friendly and exceedingly witty fellow whom we all liked to have at any sort of a party, but particularly at dinner where he could be counted on to keep the ball rolling. He did not entertain at all himself because he had only the use of a small wing of the family mansion and his father occupied the rest in taciturn disdain of the world.

The father had been served for many years by a mysterious housekeeper. He died suddenly one day and left *all* his property to her. Almost before the funeral was over, the son found his own trunks and boxes on the porch, with word that he had twenty-four hours in which to take them away.

He was exceedingly well-educated, had never been fast nor spent more money than his father had allowed him; but he had never worked, and now, while he was still under the shock of the death and the unexpected disinheritance, he was being treated without the least consideration by the intruder.

Before we had finished reading in the Newport *News* the story of his having thrown himself in front of a train, Mrs. Fish and I each received a letter from him, thanking us for our hospitality, which he had always hoped, he wrote, to repay. Then he wrote of his intention to kill himself at once. He had stopped in at the Reading Room only to write these two letters.

There was not one among us who would not have come to his aid. Mr. Fish, who had always liked him, was deeply moved when he said that he could easily have found employment for him.

CHAPTER X

THE BALL-ROOM

BALLS, LIKE STRATEGY, OUGHT TO BE STUDIED BEFORE, during and after the event. No one can predict the success of a ball, nor even judge of it while it is going on—since everyone is trying to look happy, no matter how bored one is, in order to seem a personal success. I never knew but one woman who did not pretend to talk or show animation if she did not feel it; that was Mrs. Elisha Dyer. Some said that that was because she was a Patterson—one of that Baltimore family into which Napoleon's brother had married. Mrs. Fish said that it was because she came to parties to get rested.

We had at Newport nearly all the different kinds of balls which had been described by Madame Girardon in 1848: the *"bal grandiose, bal de vanité, bal de garçon, bal d'occasion ou de voyageur, bal de cour, bal forcé, et bal d'enfant."*

We even had an American replica of the *bal de cour*—an exceedingly democratic one when the Crown Prince of Sweden arrived on a Swedish cruiser, the *"Filgia."* We tried to entertain him as royally as possible, but he insisted, as he was leaving, that he had the best time when he went uninvited with Elisha

Dyer, Harry Lehr and some of his suite to the ball
which the Swedish "help" of Newport was giving the
crew of the *Filgia*—which might be called a *bal de voyageur*. It was given at the hall of the Y.M.C.A. For my
Swedish maid it was a *bal grandiose;* she came home
with eyes shining: she had danced with His Royal
Highness!

Some of the balls at Newport stand out like jewels
in that setting of sea, moonlight and scented gardens.
Fancy dress balls were often favored by hostesses
who preferred to have the guests share the responsibility for the success or failure of the affair. It depended, then, upon their imagination whether or not
the final impression was favorable. Added to that was
the innate love of acting in all of us and the ball became a sort of escape for the members of a group who
knew each other almost too well to find continuous
pleasure in meeting, night after night.

The "triumvirate" or the "Social Strategy Board"
was made up of Mrs. Fish, Mrs. Oelrichs and Mrs. Belmont, who all loved to entertain, yet the entertainments themselves were in reality far more sober than
in the days when Mrs. Astor startled the world with
the elegance of her balls.

Until Ward McAllister, just before the Civil War,
arrived on the scene with the idea that he was born to
keep society up to a standard which—he never seemed
to realize—it had attained without his help, balls were
usually given only for debutantes. In those days the

older people danced with an air of condescension in order to hide their own pleasure!

When Frederick Martin—who was accused of staying single so that he would always be in demand for week-end parties—wrote his memoirs, he called Ward McAllister "a handsome double of Napoleon III" and he said "his winter balls will be remembered as being wonderful parties, where those present were solely selected on account of their birth and position." Freddy Martin might have added that, although you never saw or heard of Mrs. McAllister, it was her money which made him go about organizing "society."

He would have been supremely shocked at Mrs. Fish's Mother Goose ball—with its jollity and informality—at "Crossways." Yet he did permit a Mother Goose ball for the younger set—for my mother went to it.

This was one of the great winter events given by the F.C.D.C. which, being interpreted, was the Family Circle Dancing Class, a most proper and exclusive group in old New York, sponsored by mothers of debutantes, and in reality by Ward McAllister who had, as well, the last word as to what guests could be invited by the members to the very famous "Patriarchs' Balls."

He did take his self-assumed responsibilities with a deadly seriousness that none of his successors could ever achieve. He never made malicious remarks. He coined a phrase which makes me believe he must have been without a sense of humor: "Brains before Beauty and Mind before Money."

He was of a good family himself but was willing to act as a sort of grand vizier to those who gave the dinners and balls where his advice was asked. On one occasion he was complacent enough to supply the wine for a luncheon to which he had not been invited. Had he then been alive I doubt if he would have permitted that famous ball whose consequence was the self-imposed exile of the Bradley Martins—Freddy's brother and his wife.

It was a famous *bal grandiose* given in New York in the heart of a financial depression—invitations had been sent out for a fancy dress party to be given at the Waldorf-Astoria, transformed for that one night into a sort of Château of Versailles.

When, the day after, the storm broke in the American press, Mrs. Bradley Martin, says her brother-in-law, insisted that she had had the idea of a ball as a means to helping trade. And, as the invitations were sent too late for the guests to get their costumes from Paris—as they usually did—it may be that New York dressmakers benefited.

Yet that gold inlaid armor which Oliver Belmont wore, and which had cost him ten thousand dollars when he found it in Europe, did not help trade very much, nor did the authentic Pocahontas costume which the Indians had made, some time previously, for Anne Morgan.

Bradley Martin himself had appeared as a magnif-

icent Louis XV, his wife as a very sumptuous Mary
Stuart, not wearing the famous ruby necklace she possessed which had been made for Marie Antoinette, but
the equally famous diamond grape-cluster that had belonged to Louis XIV; for security she always had it
sewed to her gown when she wore it.

After the newspaper outburst against the hard-heart-
edness of giving a ball such as this in hard times, it
was the tax collector who made the situation difficult
for the Bradley-Martins. He acquired the idea—and
held on to it—that the hosts, because of the brilliance
of the affair, must be immensely more wealthy than
anyone had guessed. Their taxes were raised to such
an extent that they packed up and went to England
where their daughter, the Countess of Craven, lived.
They left the country which Bradley Martin's grandfather had defended against the British, for it was he
who had forged that chain which was hung across the
Hudson in 1776 and kept the British frigate *Vulture*
from going upstream to attack the towns along its
banks. It was from this grandfather that the fortune
had come.

A ball given in Berlin by our ambassador there,
Charlemagne Tower, stands out as one of the most
striking ones in my own experience, for I did not know
of the Bradley Martin's ball except by hearsay. The invitations for the Berlin ball stipulated that no costume
could be worn except those which had been or could
be worn to a court ball; there must be no Pierrots or

Columbines, no dominoes or imaginative disguises, sailors, etc., and no one was allowed to represent a German emperor or empress.

It was this limitation which made the ball brilliant beyond comparison. There were five in our party and we were staying together—as we had travelled together —at the old Grand Hotel; the Adlon was not yet finished. This party was a pendant to the court event, hence its formality. There were guests present who were wearing the authentic costumes of their ancestors, together with the jewels which had belonged to them.

It was at this ball that Gladys Vanderbilt, who with her mother, was of our party, met the Szechenyis, uncle and nephew. They were dressed in marvellous Magyar uniforms, she was in Roumanian costume. When Roumania and Hungary danced together they made a colorful picture! Another famous international match was made.

Mrs. Vanderbilt went as a court lady of the time of Louis XIII, in white satin cuffs and collar of deep pointed lace, gloves with jewels set in the backs—a costume hardly to be taken for that of the Empress Josephine as another guest at that ball has written in a recent book. Mrs. John Drexel wore a costume of the court of Louis XV and I went in one copied very exactly—not from one of Queen Elizabeth (as the same author has written) but from a portrait of the Pompadour whose brocaded silk and numerous ribbon bows ought to have identified it. Harry Lehr went as a Chinese Emperor in gorgeous yellow satin, heavily embroidered.

But one of the most imposing figures at this ball was the British ambassador in the long red silk robes of the Order of the Bath with collar and chain. For years he had not had any sort of fancy dress, yet he had to conform to the spirit of the party, so he obtained Royal permission to wear this costume which, of course, must never be worn as a "travesty." He went about all evening explaining that it was not as a travesty that he was wearing it, but by Royal Grant.

We had been told to note the costumes of the royal princes so as to recognize them when we began to dance. I looked hard at all of them, determined to make no blunder but, later in the evening, one of them, Prince Adalbert, the Emperor's third son, took off the long coat trimmed with fur which had hidden a blue and silver costume. He was, so far as I was concerned, absolutely unrecognizable, for I had in my zeal for impressing upon my mind the clothes forgotten to look at the faces of the princes.

Among all the brilliant balls which I can recall, the one which stands out as the most beautiful was one where a great staircase presented itself as you entered the outer door. On either side of you, as you mounted, were men in exquisite Persian costume, holding up flambeaux, whose flickering lights cast shadows upon the costumes or brought out their colors, transporting you by that simple play of torches to another world

THE BALL ROOM IN LADY DECIES' PARIS HOME

before the ballroom was entered. This ball was given
by the Comte de Castellane and the Comtesse who had
been Anna Gould. The French genius showed in the
costumes of the guests who belonged to the old noblesse and had the inimitable heritage of court manners.

While gaiety is supposed to be the keynote of the
fancy dress ball there is a bit of dialogue—we have all
heard it—which suggests that men are not always so enchanted by it:

"I'm Appius Claudius," says one of the masqueraders to his friend, who replies:

"Oh, are you? I'm unhappy as Richard Cœur de
Lion."

Usually it is the woman who chooses royal disguise
and has to be content with less noble escorts. I think
they enjoy shining against the modest backgrounds
made by the men.

I was at one ball where the man who entered dressed
as Henri IV, white plume and all, was accompanied
by his wife in a Norman peasant costume. They were
amazed to hear themselves announced as, "Mr. Henry
Carter and an enormous Pheasant."

"Alice of the Breakers" as we called Mrs. Vanderbilt, once appeared as "Electric Light." Shining too
was that costume which made the eternal fame of one
party given just after the Civil War by Mrs. Pierre
Lorillard Ronalds, "the Patti of the Salons." She had
the startling idea of having her gown embroidered

with the full score of an Italian ballet. How easily her guests could have danced to her had she been willing to turn about for the orchestra to read the music from bosom and thigh.

Her crowning glory, however, was a tiara of musical notes set about a harp, and the harp itself was illuminated by tiny gas-jets which flickered merrily above her brow; the gas-tank was carefully hidden in the thickets of her black hair! Everyone was relieved when she had the prudence to take off the tiara—and the tank, while dancing!

Years after, says Frederick Townsend Bradley, Mrs. Ronalds went to a ball at the Duchess of Devonshire's, where she repeated her earlier success. This time, however, since the science of lighting had progressed she could use electricity to illumine her harp—concealing the battery in her hair—which may or may not have been as luxuriant as before. The electric lights had the added charm of burning longer; at half past four in the morning they were still going whereas the gas-lights of the first appearance had flickered out by midnight!

Not all balls are gay; they used to be quite serious affairs for younger persons who wanted to prove themselves worthy of a second invitation from Mrs. Astor.

"I invite young people to my balls. I like to have them come," she used to say, "but they must look after themselves."

The ballroom in New York ran at the back of the two houses occupied by her son and herself; doors opening from it into their respective halls, so that only by going through the ballroom could you go from one house to the other. The staircases, however, were separated by a wall, and after Mrs. Astor's death, when her son was transforming the two houses into one, we expected to see them become one broad and magnificent flight.

Mrs. Fish and I went to see the new hall; it was now, as Mr. Astor announced proudly, "a patio" with arcades about three sides of it. The stairs were most inconspicuous. The floor to which he called our attention was done in tiles he had brought from Segovia. In the center of the patio was a large fountain. With an air of pride, he waited for us to express our admiration.

"Beautiful!" said Mrs. Fish, her head on one side, "Beautiful! Just the sort of watering-trough you might put up for a favorite horse!"

CHAPTER XI

THE CLIMBER

THERE WERE TIMES WHEN, LOOKING OUT AT THE strange procession of men and women filing through the social events of a season, I would not have minded seeing a medieval artist painting them around some wall—not necessarily a cemetery wall—as a modern danse macabre. All the elements were there.

For example there was the Climber.

She sold shoe-strings and cravats and collar-buttons in a small shop which belonged to her father. That is where her future husband met her. She must have known who he was, everybody in town did. But as he was very awkward and unpopular he probably felt grateful when she smiled at him. And he had just been refused by a girl in his own set who had laughed at him when he proposed. The pretty little shop-girl got him on the rebound.

When he told his mother she did not, to his surprise, make any blunder by forbidding the banns; she went very pleasantly to call upon the young lady and her parents.

"Henry will not be likely to find anyone else," she said, "and they seem to be very nice simple people

without any other end in view than the happiness of
their daughter.

"But, of course," she added, "they cannot be married
from the shop."

So she threw open her own house for the wedding
after having sent her own dressmaker to the mother,
her husband's tailor to the father of the bride. And
then she settled five thousand dollars a year on her son
and his wife—which was not a small amount at that
time. For I distinctly remember when I was a child and
my father and I were coming back from the Academy
of Music, asking, "Who lives down that street?" And
his saying: "Those are all rich people on that street;
there is not one of them who does not have at least six
thousand dollars a year."

She rented a house for the young couple to live in
and furnished it in cretonnes, "because flowers are so
cheerful." She had given them fire-screens like enormous fans and put pedestals wherever there was a corner not already occupied by a curio cabinet, a what-not
or étagère.

This was a good beginning for the little shop-girl
bride.

But it did not satisfy her. For there they sat at home,
evening after evening, while her husband's younger
brother and his new bride were being entertained by
all the families of their group. Nothing could be done
about it, however. It was simply that society was not
accepting them.

Fortune, however, seemed to be on their side after all, for her father-in-law died; coming into their share of the estate they could now move to New York, and start afresh on a much larger scale.

But to be quite sure of making no blunders, they engaged as social secretary a young man who had everything but money. They paid him more a year than they had had to begin with; they even gave him his own carriage and servant. Then they sat themselves at his feet to learn how to subjugate New York. As he was clever and they had the means of giving most sumptuous affairs, they got into society—or, at least, over the edge. Very soon they had a house at Newport whose Louis XII hall had lions—gilt lions—going this way and that on a buckram or gunny-sacking background of dark green. In one corner the Climber cherished a Dutch yoke, such as are used by the milkmen of Holland; in the two milk-pails were flowering plants! She had a Louis XV ballroom, and one drawing-room was Moorish.

But although the little shop-girl owed her success to their gentlemanly mentor, how she did treat him! I used to ask myself if she tried purposely to humiliate him—just because he was better-born and better-bred than she was!

"Freddy," she called out to him during a luncheon party, "will I have to go into the kitchen myself and tell the chef that this meat is not tender?"

Freddy, extremely embarrassed, assured her that he

would speak about the meat.

Another time when there were guests present she sent along the table to him a slip of paper with tags of ribbon and narrow lace on it:

"That is the list of errands that I want you to do this afternoon," she said. "First of all, go to see about the children's school clothes, then get the lace at Stern's —it is the only place you *can* get it—and then buy some more of that ribbon . . ."

"Yes, yes, I understand," said the young man, thrusting the samples into his pocket, his face flushed with embarrassment that his duties should be heralded to the world as those of an upper servant. But she kept on until she had exhausted the details and her guests.

"Freddy, did you send flowers to Mrs. H.?"

"I sent a big bouquet of violets," he said.

"Violets!" she cried. "How many times have I told you never to send violets to a sick room. They have a pestiferous smell after a few hours. Violets!"

The Climber had her husband's crest adorning the newel-post of a staircase, which looked so like one for an ocean liner that Harry Lehr once went up to the gallery above and called down:

"Stewardess, where is my cabin?"

The coronet below the crest had electric lights for "pearls." She gloried in all this.

Yet she felt absolutely sure of her popularity and went about happily unconscious of the amusement she caused. "Everyone likes me," she said, "because I never gossip and I'll play anything from bridge to puss-in-the-corner."

She came to dinners wearing diamond stars across her increasingly ample bosom and her gown embroidered with others. Turquoises, too, were her pride; she had huge ones, wearing them one night at dinner when she was seated next to a distinguished foreigner who most politely admired them.

"I can't wear them on my bare neck," she told him—and all the other guests—"because I have so much alkali in my perspiration."

And then, before he had recovered from this confidence at which everyone was smiling, she went on: "I very nearly missed this dinner because my feet had swelled so." There was an audible gasp around the table. "But I sat with them in hot vinegar for an hour," she added smilingly, "then I could get my slippers on."

Undoubtedly those slippers were too small to begin with, for she hated to order a size larger of anything, no matter how foot or form expanded.

"You make my dresses the same size as last year," she would say to her couturière, "and I'll engage to get into them."

She looked like a trussed fowl.

Yet she had small patience with other women who tried to keep their "line" by dieting, and one day, when her cakes had been refused by her guests, she threatened to have them made of wax.

"What shall I do with these?" she asked, pointing

to the profusion of uncut cakes. It was a purely ora-
torical question but . . .

"I'll take them," said one of the guests who was a
popular "hanger-on."

One night at a very formal dinner she stroked the
cloth with her two hands and then said: "They have
very nice table-linen, haven't they?"

"But what did you expect?" asked the amused person next her.

"Oh, I always feel the table-linen," she said, quite
unconscious of the chill she had produced.

Yet she had never sold table-linen in that little shop.
She was not disloyal to this past of hers, for when she
went shopping she always said to the floor-walker:

"I want a lady to wait on me."

And he would call out: "Send a lady over here to
wait on this customer."

"Physically," the Climber said another time to a
room full of people, "I'm all right. But mentally I'm
not quite all there, so I am going to Homburg."

"Why Homburg?" asked someone.

"The King is there taking his baths," she answered.

"You expect to see a lot of him then?"

"Oh, yes," she said, "I've ordered golf skirts and all
that sort of thing. I always have clothes like that when
I am doing intimate things with kings."

And how she did prefer large words: she announced
with horror one day that there had been a "rodent" in
the house.

"What is a rodent?" asked one of the group who never missed a chance to draw her out.

"Rodents," she replied, toploftily, "belong to the rat family."

One day the Climber got onto a street-car and found my mother there.

"Oh, dear!" she said, "this is the first time in my life I have ever been in a street-car."

Which statement, in view of her beginning in life, seemed surprising. Then she looked helplessly about, "What must I do to pay for the ride?"

My mother, pointing to the small box behind the driver's seat, "You must put a five-dollar bill in that little slot."

Ah, but she didn't; she dropped in the usual nickel.

Her questions used to rouse the worst in Mrs. Fish, as, for instance, how many laundresses she employed.

"I have six white ones who work all day," said Mrs. Fish, "and six black ones who work all night, only, being black, you can't see them."

Another time, she asked just how large Mrs. Fish's house was.

"I really can't tell you how big it is," said Mrs. Fish, "because it swells at night."

"Well," said the Climber, "it is the largest small house that I have ever seen."

"And yours," said Mrs. Fish, "is the smallest large house I have ever seen."

Mrs. Fish once asked a question of her own: "What

does your groom of the Chambers do? I have never had one."

"He arranges the letter-paper in the guests' rooms," replied the Climber, "and sees that the flowers are changed every day."

Going one day to a lawn-party at her Newport villa, I was impressed by a mass of pink flowers on the wire netting around the tennis court with no green about them. When I got nearer I saw they were climbing roses on a wire netting—but not a leaf! The Climber had had her gardeners busy for days clipping off every leaf!

CHAPTER XII

BRIDGE

AS MUCH AS I LOVE CEREMONY SO MUCH DO I HATE bridge. It came in, as a habit not to be shaken off, about the time I was grown. It assumed a place in the drawing-room which it has never surrendered; it is the one biggest reason why there is no longer any conversation.

I do not play bridge; I sometimes play chess which, I am sure, demands quite as much intelligence. I refuse to be scolded for a bad bridge game, to lose other people's money, or to keep quiet for hours on end and make everyone else keep quiet. The hush over a room where bridge is going on is one of the strangest silences in the world.

It must be that the game itself is to blame; even the prolonged hours devoted to it seem peculiar—set apart. Guests playing bridge are inevitably late to dinner, going up to dress only when the non-playing guests are already waiting for dinner to be served.

I knew one good player who prided himself on being a perfect gentleman. He rose at the end of a game lost by the play of a partner who was not his equal, and said with icy politeness:

Brown Brothers, photo.

"CROSSWAYS," MRS. FISH'S NEWPORT HOUSE

Now Mrs. Morris de Peyster's

"Madam, if you were a man, I would shoot you!"

As for a sense of humor, the true bridge-player loses whatever he has. Mrs. Astor and I were taking lessons from the same bridge teacher, and one day she was startled by hearing her say, her voice full of horror:

"My dear Mrs. Astor, you have trumped your partner's ace!"

"Oh, did I?" said Mrs. Astor, completely unruffled, "Well, that just makes the winning so much surer, doesn't it? We both get something!"

The teacher never smiled; she looked coldly upon me because I had enjoyed the moment.

I used to think that I had to give bridge parties even though I did not play. One day when the game was going on in its morbid hush, I wandered into a little room where, thank Heaven, thought I, there was no bridge table. There, walking up and down, wringing her hands and crying, was one of my guests, a young girl.

"What is the matter?" I cried.

"There is nothing left for me to do but kill myself," she answered in a perfect frenzy. "I have lost three hundred dollars, and I haven't the money to pay it with!"

She was not making the scene to impress me since she had had no reason to believe I would be coming into this room where she had fled in her terror. But since, in my own house, I could hardly stand there and hear a pretty girl threatening suicide because she had

accepted a foolish invitation from me to play bridge—
a game I would not play—I told her I would pay the
debt and to stop crying and walking about.

I must admit, however, that few hostesses have any
such sense of compunction; it is the game itself, I imagine, which hardens them. There was Mrs. M.—famous
already for lack of heart—who urged a young attaché
of a foreign embassy visiting her to make a fourth at
one of her tables in the country.

He demurred, saying quite frankly: "I don't play
bridge because I cannot afford to lose. I really haven't
the money to lose."

She kept right on insisting until he finally yielded,
convinced, I believe, as we all were, that she meant to
carry him and pay for him in case he lost.

An hour or two later I saw him leave the table, white
as a sheet. I took it only as his embarrassment at having to admit that he had lost. I expected to hear her
tell him not to give it a thought; it would have meant
nothing to her to pay it. But oh, no! He had lost a
year's salary and she did not say a word!

We were all furious, but she ignored our remarks,
did not pretend not to hear them but did not make
any answer. He had to pay—and every farthing! How
and where he raised that money, how he must have
pinched and sacrificed to repay it, we never knew.

But after that, whenever he was asked to play bridge,
he always said that he did not know how. Only in that
way was he sure of not being urged to play.

Oliver Belmont, who did not like bridge, used al-

ways to say when it was suggested: "I can't find the
cards. I don't believe that there is a pack of cards in
the house."

And there you have it! No one dares to come right
out and say: "I don't want to play bridge because I
don't like it."

It casts a spell on all of us. Before the game begins
all the players are terrified at the thought of what they
may lose. After the game is over, some are full of consternation at what they had lost and the others are
trying, unsuccessfully, to hide their wicked triumph at
what they have won. The air is frigid. Then you hear
floating about those detached phrases: "You should
have revoked, my dear," or "If I had known that we
were going to play . . . ," and so on and on. Social in-
tercourse has now gone completely under, it seems, and
people have to glue themselves to the chairs, assume
those peculiarly blank faces and—play bridge!

Yet I would like to know what the spell is. What is
the power behind the game which can make people sit
silent as the tomb for hours, their lips sealed tight? I
have seen bridge-players refuse to lift their eyes as a
bird-like boat swept over the line in a yacht race—
which they had come to watch!

It is a pity that Molière did not have bridge for a
subject of one of his devastating plays. But I suppose
that if they had played bridge in the time of Louis XIV
as we are playing it now, even French civilization
would have gone under long before the Revolution!

CHAPTER XIII

THE ICEBERG AND THE AVENGER

THE WOMAN WHO DID NOT PAY THAT GUEST'S DEBT AT cards was created, it would seem, to play the rôle of the Social Iceberg. It was not alone her love of cards which had stemmed the warm blood in her. She did, to be sure, play all day on Sunday and nearly every Sunday in the year. But it was her pride of intelligence which had chilled what was left of her after her pride of family had frozen her human marrow.

All the women in her family, her mother and her daughters, might have belonged to the reigning house of the Snow Queen. She and her two daughters used to stand at the top of that grand staircase, to receive their guests for a cotillion. You were chilled as you mounted. In an adjoining room you would have to greet her equally imposing mother, who was never known to unbend.

At these balls as at all others the women who did not have a partner or could not get one had to leave—that was the custom everywhere. But only at this house were they forced to go down under the eyes of their hostess; there was no other way, no private staircase, no dumb-waiter—which would have been welcomed—

no fire-escape, nothing but this conspicuous retreat after a failure to get a partner.

"It is odd," said Cousin Alice, "how men will eat your salt and then be blind in a ball-room."

What some women had to suffer going down under that sardonic smile, going down while other and hopeful guests were mounting! And then, pretending to high spirits, no matter how they felt, to wait in the dressing-room with the later comers powdering their noses, for the carriage to be announced which should remove them from their humiliation.

Nor did this Lady of the North keep this icy air just for her own house; she spread it abroad whenever it was possible. One day I was at a house where the owner had built a new big room to receive his guests more comfortably; we were all expressing our appreciation of it when in walked the Iceberg with one of her Ice Maiden daughters and several men. She stood there and looked about her in silence, then—for she always talked slowly and distinctly like a First Primer:

"What a large room. I don't like large rooms. Come, let us go home."

And they turned and went out without another word—not even a one-syllable word.

The garden, where all the rose-vines had had their leaves picked off, was not the only one to remain in my memory because of its absurdity; there was the one where the lady of the manor had had her gardeners set out growing plants in the shape of beetles; their eyes—those horrible, protruding eyes—were made with the bottoms of soda-bottles. The gardeners pushed the jagged edges of the broken bottle down into the earth and let the thick bulbous glistening ends serve for eyes!

This woman felt herself very original and an authority upon many arts. She looked at a new house for a long time one day and then made the pronouncement from the depths of her conclusion:

"I don't like it! It needs pinnacles for architectural style."

We had all believed her the soul of friendliness; we had even felt it a shame to be amused when she used to warn us:

"When you go to the Casino don't eat mushrooms, or you will be poisoned!"

She forced us to change our opinion.

A young girl, of whom we were fond, had the misfortune, while driving a new horse, to knock down and kill the husband of this lady. He was very deaf, had not heard the approaching gallop, nor seen that the horse had taken its bit in its mouth and was out of control. The girl herself was exonerated of all blame by the court and she certainly roused our sympathy for she suffered terribly at the idea of what she had done.

But the widow took no account of this grief, and I saw her, one day, several months afterwards, standing below a piazza where the girl was seated and staring so

Brown Brothers, photo.

THE CASINO AND BELLEVUE AVENUE, THE FASHIONABLE SHOPPING CENTER OF NEWPORT

malevolently at her that at last she got up and left.

Then the Avenger hissed: "I'fe hounded her out of New York and I'fe hounded her out of Newport, and I shall hound her until she dies!" (Which certainly wasn't true!)

This attitude of vengeance did not, it seems, interfere with her successful spiritualistic séances. The "spirit" of her husband often joined her in her dressing-room, she said, and told her what to wear to dinner.

"And what does *he* wear?" asked Mrs. Belmont.

"He wears red," she answered.

"Because he is in hell?" asked Mrs. Belmont.

"Because he was murdered!" hissed the other.

Mrs. Belmont always asked questions like that. She did not believe in "spirits" although I must admit that one night at "Brookholt" she came into my room and snapped on the light—looking as though she had seen a ghost.

"I hope you are not asleep yet," she said, "but that man is scratching at my window."

"What man?" I asked, sitting up in a fright and picturing burglars.

"The man who died in my room after he fell from the scaffolding outside."

I had always wondered at her sleeping in that room since I knew she had had it expressly arranged, when she built the new wing, to be her bedroom, as she wanted to sleep in a room in which no one had ever died—an idea which filled her with horror. "Brookholt," when she bought it, was so old that she felt it probable many of the rooms had known death.

Yet, in spite of the fact that death had entered the very room chosen to avoid it, she had not given it up, but slept in it. Feeling a little weird myself, I tried to assure her that since the man had died *in* the room he would not be scratching to get in but to get out: even that was not very comforting.

Houses were her passion! And she was fickle; no sooner had she finished doing over one than she would buy another. There was "Toyland," "Beacon Towers," "Brookholt," and a half dozen others. And to each one she gave both her time and her money extravagantly.

One day she spoke of a house she had just bought, to Bridget McGowan, who, from having been many years a nurse in the family, held a sort of honorary housekeeper's position. Mrs. Belmont was very fond of her and usually told her of her enterprises.

"Another house, Mrs. Belmont," said Bridget, quite downcast. "Why don't you build your mansions in the sky?"

"Because," replied Mrs. Belmont, *"I* am going to live in *your* mansions when I get there."

And then, as Bridget, who was deeply religious, looked startled,

"When I get up there, I am going to say to St. Peter, 'Where are Miss McGowan's mansions? She has been living for years in mine and now I want to live in hers.'"

Bridget looked more startled than ever, and Mrs. Belmont went on:

"They ought to be marvellous mansions, Bridget, that you have built up there, working for the good of others, giving your money to the poor and to the church, marvellous mansions!"

I thought it was wonderful!

Mrs. Belmont had the ideal red and gold lacquer tea-house on the cliffs of "Marble House" at Newport. She had Chinese come all the way from China to build it and she paid them fabulously. The little structure was gorgeous and it was authentic, but there was no place in it for the making of tea! That had to come from the house, which was a long way off. That tea could be served really hot, Mrs. Belmont had had a track laid to run from the pantry to the tea-house—it was hidden in its course by a hedge and bushes. The footmen got in the car with their trays and rode to their goal on the cliffs.

She would have made a great general if her strategy had been in demand.

Another idea of hers was the steel table in her kitchen, which she believed eminently practical even though it was hard to keep polished and rusted easily in the damp climate of Newport, Spring and Winter. But she made everyone who was planning a kitchen come and look at it.

In that same kitchen she had a chef who was made for commerce. Mrs. Belmont, who appreciated him as a cook, was only awakened to his other qualities one fall when the Pembroke-Joneses, dining with her again late in the season and being served rice-birds for dinner, asked if these were not some of the ones which they had sent up every week from their place at Wilmington, South Carolina.

No, indeed, said Mrs. Belmont, her chef had imported them, specially. This was rather disconcerting, and the Pembroke-Joneses, making inquiry at the express company's office, not only found that those birds which they had sent had been received but had been delivered to Mrs. Belmont's chef—and not merely those birds, but all the others which had been coming up from Wilmington once a week during the entire season. They had thought it rather odd not to hear from Mrs. Belmont.

They told her, and that was how she found out that all summer she had been paying the highest market price for those weekly rice-birds.

CHAPTER XIV

HANGERS-ON

HANGERS-ON MIGHT BE DESCRIBED AS THOSE WHO HAVE
learned how to live on nothing a year. The fact that
since it is human nature to want to be the center of an
admiring circle, it is almost a necessity for those who
have climbed into society to be surrounded by a court;
otherwise they would not know that they had arrived
at the desired goal.

The yacht, the country-house, are peculiarly adapted
to the holding of court. The yacht does not accommodate many and they must all be names of importance
which are announced to the world as those of guests
upon the *Nirvana* or the *Minnie-May*.

The country-house in America which becomes so
easily the château of France, is extensible; there is
room for all the Hangers-on who know their small-
talk, do not gossip disagreeably and can be counted
upon in all those lapses which even in the best-planned
programs are inevitable. The Hanger-on can be relied
upon to entertain the guest who is heavy upon the
hands of the host but who must nevertheless be kept
feeling happy so that his name may appear again as
having spent the week-end at this or that climber's

beautiful place at Newport, or the country-house.

Hangers-on are also a necessity to the hostess who, having started out the season full of energy, has filled her house with guests who count upon being amused and have no other resources than those she can offer in the way of entertainment. No matter how experienced she is, no matter how much success she has always had, there are times when she is ready to fall by the wayside. It is then that she is more than glad to have someone under obligation to her who will carry out some plan or project, taking the responsibility if it fails, giving it to her and her "gift of entertaining" if it succeeds.

The Hangers-on, who are in demand, are more often men than women, for it is not so easy to call upon a woman to be a substitute. Besides, her success may arouse jealousy, she may become over-confident, nor can she be "devoted" without seeming a sycophant, whereas a man can be as devoted as he wishes—to the persons pointed out by the hostess—and even to the hostess herself—without its seeming anything more than a tribute in perfectly good taste.

This system which permits the Hanger-on is not to be deplored; how else would impecunious young men ever have a good time—granting that they come of a good family—if it cost what it used to to go out in Society? They know their value now, it is so generally and generously allowed that they do more than their share in saving a party from inanition that they do not have to suffer any qualms as to their dignity. Even the occasional bouquet to the hostess who has "put them up" for week-ends is no longer demanded. The hostess has a hothouse of her own; it would be absurd to send her flowers less beautiful—and less costly—than those with which she supplies her own salons and tables.

The Hanger-on may, from necessity, descend to what looks distinctly like grafting. But the Grafter is of all classes in society while the Hanger-on moves only in the highest circles yet stays humble. I knew, however, a Grafter who came from one of the best families in England and who stood belligerently for her right of precedence whenever she dined out or attended a reception. Yet when she left the home of Americans who had entertained her for six weeks and more—although she had been invited for only a week—they began to receive bills for gowns, hats and what not which she had run in their name!

They did not want to make this imposition public because of the lady's prominence; they paid. Years after, when she wrote her memoirs it was very evident that she was making them an example of ostentatious luxury while pretending to marvel at it!

There used to be a woman who, to all appearances, was of our inner circle at Newport and in New York, who used to come to luncheons or dinners at Mrs. Fish's or at Mrs. Belmont's; she carried two bags with her, one for her cards and handkerchief, the other— much more capacious—for anything which took her fancy at table and was not too "squashy" to put into it. Nor did she limit herself to food; she carried away as many cigars or cigarettes as she dared—and she had plenty of daring.

Then there was the woman who one day came to call on me in Paris.

"Mrs. So-and-so is dead," she said.

I expressed my sympathy, knowing that they had been close friends.

"Yes, she is dead. She used to contribute ten thousand francs to my income every year. I thought perhaps you would like to take her place." And there was not the flicker of an eyelash.

But the involuntary hospitality of one hostess I know has always seemed to me to cap the climax of any experience under this head of grafting; it is even more ludicrous than that of my cousin, Mrs. Van Renssalaer, whose stables, during an entire hunting-season, harbored several horses of whose existence there she had no idea, but for whose food and lodging and grooming she paid. And the owner boasted of having imposed them upon her. "I couldn't have afforded to keep them otherwise," he said.

The woman in question had a large house and an elevator to the floor where the guests' rooms were. She had invited a man and his wife to spend a fortnight with her and had given them two bedrooms, each with bath, and a little salon on the floor above her own bedroom suite and boudoir. They had a son, just

back from a trip around the world, who was to stay at
a small hotel nearby so that they could see something
of him. Indeed the father explained that, if his hostess
would permit it, Edgar would come in occasionally to
dress in their rooms, as many of his clothes were in the
same trunk as his father's.

It seemed a devoted family; every evening just before bedtime the father would excuse himself, saying
he wanted to go over to the hotel and have a chat with
Eddie. And as he might be late in coming back he
would say goodnight now. Then he would go out and
his wife would go upstairs.

Their breakfast was served in their salon and was
whatever they wanted to order; they ate a hearty breakfast, they said. *They seemed to;* the cook was not used
to preparing such sumptuous breakfasts: hash or chops,
fish or omelette, toast and jam, a very large pot of coffee
was always specified. "We drink two big cups apiece,"
said the father.

The visit stretched to six weeks, but at last they left.
A few days later the hostess found in her mail a letter
for the son; not having his forwarding address, she
went over to the little hotel and asked them to send
the letter on to him.

The clerk looked at her blankly: "We have never
had anyone of this name staying here," he said.

She insisted that the son of guests of hers had spent
six weeks there; his father used to come over nearly
every evening to see him.

"You mean that young man who used to come in here and sit every evening until his father came for him? He never had a room here. He was stopping with you."

That is why it is necessary to keep in mind the elevator which was in the hall to one side of my friend's house and opened on the hall leading to the guests' rooms and nowhere else. Not even the servants had guessed that instead of two visitors there had been three. Had father and son gone up the stairs the servants would have heard them, but, stepping quickly into the elevator from the outer door, not saying a word until they arrived at their rooms, they were quite safe.

Hospitality to be real has to be consciously offered and conscientiously accepted. But to be "made use of" . . .

There is the guest who is invited to take an auto trip with you, perhaps to visit at some house where you have asked her to be invited, believing that she was harmless. And you suggest that, aside from the little suit-case which she may need for the day or two days' journey, she send her trunk on by express.

She says with a sweet smile that she only has the suit-case and a little bag; but when just as you are leaving, you find that she has had two steamer trunks pushed *into* the car, you are at a loss to know just what to say. You content yourself with hoping for the best until, the trunks being dislocated at the end of the trip,

Brown Brothers, photo.

BAILEY'S BEACH, NEWPORT

you find the lining of the car has been badly torn and
the door itself so nearly unhinged and strained that
the car—a new one which has just taken a prize at the
show—has to be sent back to the makers to be re-done.

If it were a question of expense, you would have
been only too glad to have paid the express charge, for
no matter what it might have been it could not have
been as big as the bill for the repairs to the car.

Another imposition: The man visiting a friend of
mine and using the long-distance telephone from her
house in Rome to his home in San Francisco. He used
it three times. He did not ask if he might telephone
nor say that he had telephoned. And the bill was presented only after his departure—for three hundred
dollars!

When one of Mrs. Fish's English guests once com-
plained of the hard ride to Chicago from New York
which she was not anticipating with any pleasure, Mr.
Fish offered his private railroad car to take her there.
She accepted with alacrity. Did she stop at Chicago?
No indeed!

She kept that car for two months. And she left it in
Mexico!

"That was going a little strong," said Mr. Fish, after
he had paid the mileage, the food and service bills,
and got the car back into its native land.

But that is only an exaggerated form of what happens time and again.

"Will you have someone call a cab," the guest says

—only today she would say "taxi." This is after lunch or tea. The telephone calls the cab-stand which usually serves your house guests and the bill is sent to you.

That might be taken as a matter of course. But when you find that after your lunch guest got home she kept the taxi while dressing for dinner, kept it outside the house where she dined to go to the theatre and dismisses it only at two o'clock in the morning, you do feel that you have been slightly imposed upon.

Of course you never speak of it to her. That would be "bad form." "It isn't done."

CHAPTER XV

THE EGOTIST

THE IDEAL EGOTIST, TO MY MIND, WAS A MAN I KNEW who always had his wife and daughter follow him out of the dining-room at hotels to keep the draught off his back! Oddly enough this same man owned a house which was on the windy ledge of Newport and which he had named "Bleak House," which for so sensitive a person must have been a name to make him shiver.

Another type of the self-centered is certainly the man who has his cigarette case especially stream-lined to fit the curves of his body under that pocket where he carried it.

Another one was a woman who would not, because of ill-temper, let the body of her sister-in-law's mother stay in the family vault belonging jointly to their two husbands' estates. And, although it was the middle of a New York winter and it was deadly for the horses of a hearse to have to go out to the cemetery and climb a hill, insisted that, within three days, removal should be made. And this order, threatening legal reprisals in case it was not obeyed, was cabled from Europe! So Mrs. S's body had to be removed to the receiving vault while waiting the completion of her own.

"I lost my turquoise pin at your circus-party this afternoon." Mrs. Oelrichs heard a guest say over the telephone, just after leaving her great circus-party at Newport. "Will you ask someone to look for it?"

Mrs. Oelrichs ordered a thorough search—which continued all the next day, Sunday. She also set eight women to weeding the lawn and offered a reward. She had the fountains dried, the walks and roadway raked.

For two days everything was subordinated to that search. But finally, much depressed, she went to the telephone and called up the guest and told her the brooch had not been found.

A merry laugh greeted her statement.

"Oh, my dear, I found, just after I had telephoned you, that I had not worn that pin, after all; it was in my jewel case."

But I often think that the hardest-hearted egotism was one in which I had my part. For I was one of the guests invited to meet the famous Mrs. Maybrick whom Mrs. S. had invited to come from England upon her release from prison.

The underlying wish of Mrs. S. may have been to be kind to a woman whom she insisted upon believing innocent of a murder. But the situation was no less cruel. There we were, sixteen at a formal luncheon, and the guest of honor was Mrs. Maybrick who had just arrived. For many years she had been in solitary confinement; on being released she had accepted Mrs. S's invitation and come directly to New York. And here she was, not as I suppose she had hoped to be, cared for in quiet surroundings, getting used to the very sound of voices, the very sight of what was no longer prison walls, of the mere touch of life, but thrust into the midst of a circle of curious women who, in her eyes at least, had never known what trouble was. Here she was eating with difficulty at a table whose every article must have spelled some association with that far-off time before she had been accused of the murder of her husband and sentenced to life imprisonment!

To have put her in that position seems to me to have been the height of egotism, for to do *her* any honor would have been to have respected her need for a long re-education in the world. I remember that she did not talk, that she hardly ate a thing, that she seemed to be looking out of the corners of her eyes at us. What was she thinking?

One day, a year or two ago in Paris, my maid noticed three women whom she could identify as Americans, peering into the courtyard. She saw too, on coming nearer, that they wore the gold star and at once she was the spirit of hospitality and told them this was the home of an American woman whose son had fought in the war.

Would they like to come in and visit it because the house was historic?

They would. As they were leaving she turned, full of sympathy, to one of the three and said: "I am very sorry that you lost your son in the war."

To her amazement the woman burst out laughing.

"Good lord," she said, "I've never had a son. More than that I've never been married. But I have wangled my way over three times with the Gold Star Mothers just the same!"

And before my maid could say a word she added: "What I'm hoping is that I'll find a husband on some of these trips."

CHAPTER XVI

THE BEDROOM

IT IS PROBABLY BECAUSE AS A CHILD I WANTED TO HAVE a blue bedroom and could not since my elder sister had chosen that color for hers, that I have always looked with curiosity to see what colors other women have chosen to use in their bedrooms. That I should have wanted blue when my mother—whose taste I usually adored—had pink, may have been due to the fact that I did not like the color of the carpet of her room which, she said, was "neutral" and necessary to the color scheme. Later I saw some gorgeous pink bedrooms—one belonging to Mrs. George Gould, and the luxurious one of Mrs. Leeds.

"What bliss to be in the boudoir of a luxury-loving woman!" said Boldini the artist, as he went about the room touching with sensitive fingers the silks and satins in all their rose-colored tones. Even Mrs. Leeds' bric-à-brac was in pink quartz, her toilet set done in gold—five kinds of gold. She had, too, a diamond-studded frame to keep a lock of her boy's hair in; and when she became "the world's richest widow," she had a tomb of pink marble made for Mr. Leeds.

Mrs. Belmont and I were looking at that tomb when

it was being built in Woodlawn cemetery, and re-
marking upon its probable cost, which we were told
later was, with that of all the space bought for it and
perpetual care, half a million dollars, when Mrs. Belmont, who did not care for the pink marble, exclaimed:

"Ridiculous! Absolutely ridiculous!"

A workman overheard her.

"Well," said he, "if you think this is funny, go and
look at that tomb over there where the crazy woman
who built it has put cats on the roof!"

There it was, a fine piece of workmanship, a mauso-
leum patterned after St. Hubert's chapel at the
Château of Amboise; and, just as in the original, the
roof was ornamented with stag's antlers and two very
lifelike cats of sculptured stone. We stood there and
laughed—but *not* at the cats, this tomb belonged to
Mrs. Belmont herself!

Mrs. Leeds' toilet articles were always insured at
Lloyd's; she never had the experience of coming in to
a hotel bedroom one day, as Tessie Oelrichs did, to
find that all the gold backs had been taken from the
brushes and mirrors of her toilet set, as well as the
tops of powder boxes and perfume bottles.

"I suppose," said Mrs. Oelrichs tranquilly, "that
they thought they were taking real gold—but it was
only silver gilt."

Her bedroom was always in blue while Mrs. Belmont's was usually in white. Mrs. Fish had a fine

Copyright, 1906, by W. C. Harris

MRS. STUYVESANT FISH'S GOTHIC BEDROOM

Gothic bedroom but she never slept in it; it was too perfect as a period room to seem home-like to one of her easy-going nature, so she had her bed put up in what would otherwise have been the dressing-room of this formal chamber. All her rooms were hospitable and you enjoyed sitting down in any one of the comfortable big chairs and feeling absolutely at home; it was the same in any of Mrs. Belmont's houses; she had a genius for taking all styles of furniture and putting them together without their jarring, making a "living-room" where you liked to sit on and on, talking and listening. But the excessive sense of order which ruled one woman's house cast a slight chill; if, by any chance, you happened to move a piece of bric-à-brac out of place she was sure to notice it, even while you were there, and to put it carefully back to the exact spot where it had been.

Mrs. Oelrichs set an example which we ought to have followed, for she took her responsibility seriously; every morning at nine, while others of us were still comfortably in bed, Tessie, dressed and her hair done, was going from room to room of her house seeing personally to every detail. That finished, she jumped into her little electric runabout and went to the garages and stables to look them over. She was a general reviewing her domestic troops.

Some of her staff objected—although not to her. One butler paid Mrs. Fish the doubtful compliment when he was being discharged by saying:

"At least I will say for you, Madam, that you are a lady: you never go into the kitchen as some do."

Mamie Fish was rather too easy-going, Cousin Alice thought, in the way she seated her guests and I heard her say one evening in New York as we were leaving the dining-room after a dinner of one hundred, at five tables:

"I was so near the pantry that the waiters had to pass their dishes right over my head."

"You certainly ought to have been satisfied," retorted Mamie as quick as a flash. "You not only had a dinner but a Passover too."

Poor Cousin Alice! She was so seldom satisfied with her place at table and so perfectly willing to complain about it to her host or hostess that she was quite a problem.

"Where *shall* I seat her?" one host asked himself vainly until he had gone all round the table in imagination and not found a seat to please her—for he knew, as we all did, her pretensions. Finally, his face cleared:

"I have it! She shall be in the center of the table, instead of the flower-piece. Then she cannot complain that I haven't given her the most prominent place there is."

Trying to please the guests was hard, also to run one's house well with such spoiled servants as we all had. Mrs. Fish's butler was equalled in his stern sense of the fitness of this or that behaviour by Carpenter, her housekeeper. In time Mamie grew rather tired of being corrected or having suggestions made to her, for she knew exactly what she wanted to do and why she was doing it, so when Mrs. Leeds said one day with great fervor:

"What wouldn't I give to have two such perfect servants as your butler and housekeeper!" Mamie replied, without a moment's hesitation:

"Take them!"

And she did, quite to the contentment of all concerned, for she liked a butler to feel full of responsibility and a housekeeper to relieve her of any cares as to the other servants and the running of the house, whether in London or on the Riviera.

Several years later, I was in the Princess Anastasia's box with Mrs. Leeds at the Opera in Monte Carlo when I noticed a smart grey-haired woman in the audience who had kept her seat during the entr'acte.

"That is the best coiffure here tonight," I said, pointing her out.

"Isn't it?" said Mrs. Leeds. "That is Carpenter. I send the coiffeur to her twice a week; it is really the least I can do for her."

Carpenter, Mrs. Fish's former housekeeper—and who had begun as a second housemaid—now in the lap of extreme luxury, had been raised to the position of majordomo. The hairdresser twice a week was but an item in the list of generosities accorded her; she was wearing furs and a diamond bracelet which would have been coveted by many a woman in that audience;

she had her own car and footman. In return she gave orders to the other servants as to the decoration of the rooms with flowers, the overseeing of *everything*.

Carpenter was to be seen every morning in detached dignity, going about the rooms, with a bevy of maids following her, their hands filled with vases, and she would say with an accent which time did not better:

"*Là! Mettez là!*" or, speaking to the man who did the floors:

"*Parquet, nettoyez.*"

Even that duty seemed to me to be doubtfully inadequate, for at Monte Carlo when she found that she could not rent the usual rubber-plants and palms which some early education had marked upon her memory as absolutely essential in any hall, she had bought them at Mrs. Leeds' great expense. And they were given back to the florist at the end of the season.

"If I couldn't be Mrs. Stuyvesant Fish," Mamie said one time, "I'd rather be Mrs. Leeds' secretary than anyone else."

For Mrs. Leeds had the reputation of so spoiling anyone who lived near her that life seemed a bed of roses. Of all the women who had a great deal of money at her disposal, she seemed to enjoy it the most. She loved luxury and was like a kitten on a soft down quilt. But, unlike a kitten, she wanted to include in her sense of warmth and comfort all who were associated with her. To be her secretary or one of her maids would be to revel in the good things of life—and to have few re-

LADY DECIES' BEDROOM, PARIS

sponsibilities.

She had two maids; both were devoted to her; her sweetness prevented her offending one or the other; did she give one something to do, the other stood by waiting for an equivalent order; it was a rare situation. Finally, when her marriage with Prince Christopher of Greece made it necessary for her to observe certain formalities, she raised the head maid who had been with her the longest.

This was quite an adventure for the young woman, who suddenly found herself of importance when she, travelling with "the Princess," had to wear evening dress at dinner because she would be dining with the manager of the hotel wherever the Princess was stopping, as was usual with servants of Royalty. She got used to being treated with deference by those who were accustomed to thinking of her as an equal, for servants always take the rank of their employers.

Mrs. Fish had had a secretary of her own and when she saw a book entitled "The Confessions of a Social Secretary" she bought it and read it. Under the thin veneer of "Fisher" she recognized herself and Mr. Fish as the leading characters in the story. Other disguises were equally transparent, as, for instance, Mrs. "Pemberton-Jones" for Mrs. "Pembroke-Jones."

When Mr. Fish had perused the volume he lost no time in tracing the anonymous writer of it, who proved to be their own housekeeper, a woman whom they had treated with the greatest kindness under the most dis-

tressing circumstances. Her son of twelve had been
found to be the thief who had taken the money with
which to pay the servants for the first of the month.

Yet because the boy was so young he had been forgiven and at this very time he was being educated at
Mrs. Fish's expense with a view to becoming an architect and was "visiting" her at Newport. The writer
of the "Confessions" was discharged.

Her successor had been a cashier in a hotel in a large
southern city when the family fortunes had made employment a necessity. She did not write books and was
soon considered almost as a friend with a suite of rooms
for herself, with flowers and fruits on her table, and a
servant of her own.

But after Mrs. Fish's death her solitude determined
her to leave and take a position with a recent widow,
prominent in that society which Mrs. Fish had so dominated by her personality. Here, however, she began to
gossip indiscreetly about the widow's visitors, many of
whom were assiduous admirers. She had to leave.

Her third position was with one of the *nouveau
riche,* for whom her scorn had no limit, when one day
she met me and told me her odyssey.

"She even asked *me* to ring the bell for the servant
and order a glass of water" . . . And after letting the
effect of that sink in . . .

"I told her she could ring that bell herself, that it
was not *my* place to do so."

There are, it seems, a great many advantages to be

gained by understanding the hierarchy of duties in any household. And it must be admitted that the bridging of chasms may be difficult when you are trying to educate the woman who has engaged you to be social secretary, advisor and councillor.

There are vantage points too, sometimes, from which surrounding society may be judged. There was that manicure who was successful simply because she had so much insight into people. Everyone talked to her and she listened intelligently.

She lent money to a young blade who was known to be unreliably extravagant. One day, while she was doing my nails, she told me that she had lent him all her savings.

She smiled serenely. "He is going to pay me back when his father dies and he comes into his fortune," she said.

"But what a risk," I said. "How do you know his father isn't going to disinherit him?"

The father did die very shortly after. He disinherited his wayward son. He had been cut off without a cent! Fortunately I knew the nephew and his wife who came into the fortune and I told them the story. They paid her.

CHAPTER XVII

MY MOTHER

THROUGHOUT HER LIFE MY MOTHER KEPT HER WORLD intact. It was like going into something unchangeable and serene whenever, between the season at Newport and the season in New York, I would visit my mother at Pen Rhyn. She had not married again although she had had what her friends thought were "brilliant offers." Her old rector, Dr. Houghton, had had a great influence, I am sure, on her decision to stay a widow. He had called on her again and again, after my father's death, to warn her against a second marriage, painting the dangers with a sombre brush.

"Rich widows," he said, "may be in love with the man, but the man is in love with the money,"—which was not too flattering to my mother who looked very lovely in her black and was still young.

And he never left without telling some fearful story of how a widow had been murdered by her second husband for the sake of her wealth or of how unhappy and miserable other widows were who had not been murdered. He even gave her a dire book of such tales to read at her leisure.

"It is very queer," said my mother, "but Dr. Houghton doesn't seem to know any happy second marriages at all."

I am sure that the fact that Queen Victoria had remained a widow made it easier for her to retire to the country which breathed family traditions.

At Pen Rhyn she kept on with her charitable work; it had never been corrected by any theory about talented and salaried workers being preferable to the personal contact. She used to buy from a pedlar who came along the road in front of her house, at frequent intervals. I expressed my surprise that she should buy so much linen, since she did not need it.

"As long as I do buy from him," she explained, "I like to lighten his load as much as possible. And linen is the heaviest thing he carries."

She had that linen made up into those "useful presents" to be given at Christmas time to the country people round about.

No matter what the weather was at Pen Rhyn, everyone who was invited to the Christmas tree came. Neither snow nor wind could keep them away; they assembled in numbers, although each invitation had been by name. A fir tree grown outside on the lawn was gaily decorated and surrounded with packages. My mother, wrapped in a shawl, stood in the window while one of the footmen, in Santa Claus costume, distributed the gifts. Every man, woman and child was presented with a "useful" and a "gift." That ceremony over, in they all came to have tea, hot chocolate, hot muffins or cake in the cheerful, warm and decorated servants' hall.

Nor was that state of mind entirely of the holidays. I remember her sitting on the porch of some people who lived near the grade crossing at Pen Rhyn. They had asked whether she would not prefer sitting there with them rather than to wait in the carriage with the horses restless and uneasy until the gate could be opened, after the delayed train.

How the conversation started I do not know but my mother asked the woman how things were going with her and she replied that she could be perfectly happy if she had forty dollars more a year. So my mother, on arriving home, sent her forty dollars. And kept on sending forty dollars on that same date every year, saying, "I am buying perfect happiness for forty dollars a year."

The people around Pen Rhyn had the reputation of being very honest. That honesty was confirmed by an incident which in spite of being momentarily tragic had its lighter side. My mother's carriage ran over a man's dog; she told him she wanted to repair the loss.

He replied that he would like very much to make a rug out of the red setter's skin and that it would cost five dollars. She sent him a check; one day she received a grateful letter, enclosing fifty cents.

"The rug is beautiful," he wrote, "it only cost four-fifty, so I return the change."

No matter what it was that she had to pay she paid

MRS. JOSEPH W. DREXEL, THE AUTHOR'S MOTHER

by check. That was because, living on a highroad and not having too much confidence in the purely local honesty pervading the tramps who came from distant places, she wanted people to know that she never had ready money in the house. No one ever refused the check she offered.

One time when I was there I heard her audibly enquiring for eleven dollars all over the house, with the door open so that the man waiting there could hear her. Finally she gave him a check. She had staged this appeal, she told me, because the man was "such a villainous-looking person" that she wanted to be very convincing.

She would never wear diamonds at Pen Rhyn. "They know what diamonds are," she said; "but rubies, emeralds or sapphires are 'just stones' to them and have no value."

When the swamp at Pen Rhyn was finally drained, I asked why the two-storied shack at the entrance of the grounds had not been taken away—ugly, tumbled-down, white-washed, it had been left there by the Gun Club.

"Tear that down? No, dear! It is a tramp discourager. No strange tramp going by here would believe there was any reason in appealing for help from people who had a shack like that at their gate."

A friend of ours was once complaining that a ruined castle which she had purchased could not be made comfortable in the modern way.

My mother had no sympathy for her: "Running water in a feudal castle? *I* could get along without it."

Harry Lehr used to say that she "perched like a butterfly," no matter where she was; that was true, yet it did not disturb her keen perception of the life about her for which she sometimes had a stinging criticism.

A relative of ours, who had been left a widower with two children, wrote that he had married a second time "to provide a nurse for the children." Several years later, when his family had increased each year, my mother remarked: "He has not only provided the children with a nurse, he has generously provided the nurse with children."

And another story which she used to tell with a certain pride was a sign of those times. She was entertaining a young caller in our Blue Salon:

"Would it incommode you if I smoked in here?" he asked.

"I really cannot tell you," she replied, genially. "No one ever has."

Admiring that frankness of hers, I am not displeased when I read of myself as I did a year or two ago. . . .

"She inherited from her mother, the late Mrs. Joseph W. Drexel, who was descended from the famous Wharton family, the characteristic of direct speech."

It must have been something of this same temperament in Mrs. Belmont which attracted me to her; she was not one thing to your face and another behind your back.

"Have you brought that noisy maid with you again?"
she asked when I arrived for a visit. I had indeed
brought the same maid who, to my mind, was remark-
ably quiet.

"Tell her to take her shoes off." And Mrs. Belmont
had a pattern drawn of my maid's foot on a piece of
wrapping paper. Then she went in person and bought
a pair of felt-soled slippers.

Every servant in the house wore such slippers. In the
morning my chauffeur had to come up to get his orders
for the day; the other servants would stand around
breathless while he stamped upstairs.

"I'll not go sneaking up those stairs," he said.

To avoid a possible reprimand, I sent him his orders
by my felt-footed maid.

Yet Mrs. Belmont's outspokenness never seemed to
lose her her friends as it might have done with another. I remember how annoyed she was when a guest
at the Opera tried to borrow her glasses.

"Doesn't he realize that you can catch all sorts of
contagious eye-troubles?"

So the next time she asked this man to her box at
the Opera, she presented him with a handsome pair of
glasses. "And remember always to carry them with
you," she admonished him.

Another time she heard that the servants carrying
up the trunk of a week-end visitor had torn the wall-
paper on the staircase in the single men guests' wing.

"Why do you bring a trunk when you only come for

a few days?" she asked him. "Why don't you carry a suit-case or two if you must have so many clothes?"

"I haven't any suit-case," said the poor fellow, not knowing just how to take this reproof in front of the other guests and was much relieved when everyone laughed. But when he got back to town with that guilty trunk there, waiting for him—with her card—was a handsome and capacious suit-case.

Another guest of hers smoked in bed. On his departure the housekeeper told her that the sheets had several big holes in them.

"Very good!" said Mrs. Belmont. "Have them washed and then just draw the holes together with the coarsest darning cotton you can find. When he comes again, see that he gets them on his bed."

He came again and as he was leaving he grew confidential:

"Everything is so perfect here. You have such wonderful linen, Mrs. Belmont, that I think I ought to tell you that it is not being taken care of as it should be. You ought really to see the sheets on my bed!"

"Ah, yes, those sheets!" she replied. "You're quite right. Those are the sheets you burned holes in with your cigarettes. I had them darned especially for your personal use."

Sheets were taboo in that man's presence thereafter, just as bath-towels were in another group.

For bath-towels played quite a scandalous rôle one summer at Newport, when two of our friends, unknown to the rest, stayed all night at a bungalow used only as a resting-place in the day time. No one might ever have known of the escapade however if the following morning one of them had not telephoned to the Gooseberry Island Club to send up towels. The employee of the Club, feeling his lack of authority, telephoned in turn to the President who told him to row over with them—and then it leaked out, of course.

It made quite a story of innuendos for the "Newport Nuisance" as we called the *News* because it always arrived at the hour we were dressing for dinner.

Mrs. Fish never had to dread gossip,—the open book was secretive compared to her manner of living. Yet it was just that openness which made us wonder on one occasion whether a very devoted follower was not going to prove the exception, even though she had not before given any hint of being at all impressed by his attentions. We were on the launch going out to the *Narada* for dinner; there was a wonderful moon, romance was in the air. Nevertheless we were surprised to see Mrs. Fish so evidently affected by the beauty of it all. She was sitting beside the devoted follower, and under the influence of that moon her mood was visibly changing into one of sentiment.

"How lovely this is!" she said to him. "Let me hold your hand." The rest of us gasped—as she went on laughingly: "Then I will close my eyes—and think it is someone else!"

Sooner or later she always discouraged any attempt

at paying court. One morning on the beach a man who had been trying to play the devoted beau leaned over with his usual fatuous air and picked up her gloved hand to kiss it.

It came off!

Harry Lehr had filled her glove with cold wet sand!

When she had seen the gentleman crossing the beach towards her, she had drawn her hand out of sight and held the clammy substitute just beyond the edge of her cape.

But it is always pleasing to a woman to have embryo suiters. I knew a charming widow who had several, and each one believed that *he* was to be her ultimate choice because it was his photograph, beautifully framed, which was in evidence upon a prominent table.

They were all mistaken. She had only one frame. Whenever one of her admirers was announced, she took from a drawer full of photographs his picture and slipped it into the frame. This sometimes demanded a remarkable sleight-of-hand but the genial atmosphere with which she was constantly surrounded repaid her for her trouble.

There were always a few reliable "henchmen" whose attentions were pretty evenly distributed and who were in demand in any emergency where an extra man was needed. One of these was very popular but very thrifty and liked to make a "third" if any expense was probable.

It was the custom on the rare occasions we used to

go to Coney Island to split up in twos so as to take in
only those entertainments which appealed personally.
And I remember one evening when I was there with
my escort, the thrifty one fastened on us for the occasion. Whenever my escort would say at the window:
"Two tickets, please," a voice without hesitation
would come over his shoulder: "Make it three."

We all knew he had money and that house which
he had inherited from his father. He was just naturally
of a saving disposition. He even had an occasional love
affair, although in his case it was quite literally true
that "the woman paid." Nor could she ever be pitied
for bearing the whole expense of the romance since
his reputation for thriftiness was not under a bushel.
Moreover that tendency to financial discretion covered discretion itself. He was never guilty of compro-
mising anyone. I have sometimes thought that the
gossip about his affairs had no real foundation perhaps.

One romance he might have had and benefited from
if his doctor had not abused professional secrecy and
told the bride-to-be, also a patient, that he had heart
trouble and could hardly live more than two years.

She had already been married to a man who had
been ill some time before his death; she was afraid of
having again to face that sort of tragedy. The engagement was broken—if it had really been a definite engagement. He never knew, I believe, why.

And he did die before the two years were up. His
servant found him dead in bed one morning—all alone

in that house. Perhaps had he been happily married . . .

There was a *woman* whom we all called "Sponger"
and tried our best, as a solution of her problem and
ours, to marry off. She was one of the single items of
an illustrious family. Her visits, during the season at
Newport, were as regular as clockwork. She would
begin at Mrs. Fish's.

At the end of two weeks, Mamie would say to Mrs.
Oelrichs:

"You have got to take her off my hands. I can't stand
her another day!"

And Mrs. Oelrichs would accept the burden for a
fortnight and then pass her on. We all did our share.

Not that she had any fault you could put your finger
on, unless it was the deep bass voice in which she
boasted of her ancestors and complained of her con-
temporary relatives.

"Was your bath all right this morning?" asked Mrs.
Fish.

"I didn't take a bath," she said in her profound
voice. "The tub was full of flowers from the older
men."

"There you go!" said Mamie. "Older men. Don't
make such distinctions. Look as young as you can and
never refer to age in anyone or any way!"

"If you only would not insist upon wearing so much
white!" said Mrs. Belmont. "White veils frighten the

men. You'll never get a husband unless you wear colors."

One morning one of her hostesses came to the beach in high feather. "I think I've managed it at last!" she said proudly. "She is going to be married!"

"To whom?" we cried.

"I haven't the right to mention his name," replied the jubilant lady, "because he hasn't really proposed yet. But I've been bringing them together all Summer and they are *so* suited to each other, since he has money and no family and she has family and no money."

We were spell-bound at the idea of a marriage culminating all our efforts. We insisted upon knowing the man's name. And then we were like spent balloons.

For the man who had been thrown in the way of the Sponger was already married. His wife was an invalid who never appeared at Newport. The matchmaker was probably the only woman at Newport who did not know this. Her feathers drooped.

As the season wore on, we always watched for a yacht going back to New York; then we would suggest her going up to New York that way. The owner of the yacht could, of course, do nothing but second our invitation in his name.

And she always accepted of course.

There are many more ways of getting along with little money than you might suppose. I am thinking of a woman in financial difficulties who managed to

procure herself a hazardous home in a hotel by publicity among her friends persuading them to entertain
there. It was understood by the hotel that what they
paid covered her expenses too. Most of her friends
knew this and were not to be pitied.

On one occasion this lady wanted to make a handsome wedding present and ordered a marvellously embroidered bag—a royal gift. As she already owed the
shop for several others—and all expensive—the bag-
maker told her she could only have it by paying cash;
he was willing to let the rest of the account run a while
longer.

She agreed and asked him to send the bag by a boy
directly to her room. The boy himself was told most
emphatically not to let the bag leave one hand before
he had the money in the other.

At the door he was on his guard until the woman
asked him smilingly if he had change for a thousand
francs. He had. Very well, she would get the bill and,
taking the bag from him, now quite at his ease, she
closed the door.

Then she went to the telephone, called up the door-
man downstairs and told him that there was a messenger boy who had been insolent and was annoying
her and please to have him thrown out.

He was.

I knew a dressmaker who had made clothes for certain members of an exiled royal family, and in the

goodness of her heart asked them very little; they spread her fame in their circle. So that she was not surprised one day to see another royal person, from a recently republicanized country, come in to give her an order.

When the dresses were finished, the personage was much pleased. Then the bill arrived, a modest one, for the dressmaker had small rooms at the top of several flights of stairs, and only charged accordingly.

"What!" cried the new customer. "You dare to send me a bill! You ought to be proud to work for me!"

And she never paid that bill. The dressmaker not only had to pay her girls for their work, but to pay for the material, to say nothing of her rent. But she knew no way to get the money.

Not long after, one of her wealthy customers came in, by appointment. With her was the royal lady, all smiles and bows. While the rich woman tried on certain furs, choosing several, the other tried on a fur coat, a "latest model" and was so pleased with it that she said she would keep it on. In a few moments, she left with her old one over her arm, still bowing and smiling.

The rich customer made her choice and gave her orders.

The dressmaker thought the rich American customer was giving the royal lady a present, not so.

"I have never seen her before in my life," said the lady of wealth.

One day soon after the door opened again to let in the personage who was all smiles.

"I have come in to tell you that I have sold that coat to a friend for the price you named. When she sends me a check you shall have the money at once."

Not long after the dressmaker was at a cinema and there she saw in the news-reel the distinguished silhouette of her coat upon the back of the royal personage who was *embarking for a foreign country!*

CHAPTER XVIII

CLOTHES

THERE HAVE BEEN TOO MANY WISE SAYINGS ABOUT monks and their habits, man and his clothes, for any woman to pretend that she is made by what she wears, but the rôle played by clothes is nevertheless too important for her to assume superiority to them. She wears what fashion dictates and only dares to be less daring in following its decrees after she has assured herself a place in the sartorial arena. Today when the mannequins parade in rooms whose furniture looks as though it were made out of bent hatpins, the mood is entirely different from that of before-the-war, when a certain opulence in the setting gave warmth of background to the gowns.

As for the difference between our days and those in which the seamstress came twice a year from Philadelphia to the little town where my mother lived to sew for a week—that is almost too great a gap for the imagination to bridge. My mother and her sister spent much time helping the seamstress, ripping and ruffling and talking of what was "most fashionable."

And yet later, my mother could not keep abreast of the time except by pretending to like Ferris waists and

flat-heeled shoes for her daughters—which she refused
to do. Her simplicity took itself out in the insistence
upon our school costumes; our winter clothes were cut
out of the Gordon plaid which she felt we had a right
to wear since we had Gordons in our ancestry.

It was a blue and green plaid with yellow cross-lines,
and it was, much as I sometimes deplored wearing it
year after year, the beginning of my interest in Scotch
plaids which contain within their color schemes the
whole history of clans and their traditions. And I like,
too, the rule in Scotland that no one may wear a plaid
which is not his or hers by ancient right; if he does,
it may be stripped from him or her wherever he or
she happens to be. And so deeply implanted is this
feeling for guarding their green and blue, yellow and
red combinations that even out of Scotland the sight
of a plaid where, to their mind, it ought not to be
awakens strange reactions.

The Duke of Athol! told me some years ago—for it
was when the fashion for plaids set in—that he was
fascinated by the sight of his own tartan made up
into a fashionable gown which a woman was wearing
on the Champs Elysées.

Without thinking he kept his eye upon that plaid
and found himself in a tea-room still looking at it until
the lady herself, noticing his fixed gaze, spoke uneasily
to the maître d'hotel who came to his table and re-
buked him politely for the unwanted attention he was
forcing upon her.

"But she is wearing my dress," explained the Duke. Whereupon, as he said, "Not knowing that in Scotland we call our plaid our 'dress,' they took me for stark staring mad and I had the devil of a time explaining myself."

The lady, however, was completely mollified when she learned the identity of the gentleman who had been watching her so closely.

At a luncheon in Scotland late in September where I was seated next a man in conventional blue serge at Blair Castle, I told him I was sorry to see him dressed like that when he might be wearing kilts.

"Ah, but the weather is too cold for kilts," he replied.

"But didn't your ancestors wear kilts the year round?" I asked.

"They did," he said, somewhat testily, "but they had hair on their legs."

To my youthful eyes, the bustle was a perfectly normal expression, even though I never detached it from the bulging awning for windows whose tops are rounded. And the "balayeuse" too was accepted as a natural guarantee against the dirt which trailing skirts must necessarily touch—"dust ruffle" as it was called in English and worn within any other low ruffle or even within a plain hemmed skirt.

My sister, Kate, and I differed in our attitude towards fashion; she hated, from the outset, anything which could be called "gew-gaws"; all superfluity was sentimental and superior intelligence demanded that everything, whether fashion, fact or theory, be sifted. Indeed it was quite exhausting to follow her upon the proud path she took, but if you didn't you would find that you too had been pretty thoroughly sifted and left unrecognizably diminished.

Even before my mother's love of the romantic, Kate was adamant and when she received from her after the announcement of her engagement to Dr. Penrose, an enormous bouquet of la France roses with a quill pen sticking straight up in the middle, she was indignant—just why we could not understand. The quill pen in our family was considered an essential. My mother never wrote with any other; she learned that Queen Victoria preferred them too—an expensive essential since it was Tiffany who supplied them and cut them.

"Veil and white dress!" stormed Kate, when the clothes for her wedding were being considered. "Don't you realize," she asked, with irritation, "that we are going to Hell Roaring Camp on our honeymoon, and will sleep in bags on the ground?"

They did. But Kate wore the conventional white dress and veil at the wedding just the same and she did not, as she wished, have the "Ride of the Valkyries" instead of the wedding march nor a woman preacher instead of a man for that ceremony which she said loftily "was a mere matter of form."

Brown Brothers, photo.

RICHARD T. WILSON

My mother used to get her clothes from Felix in
Paris and from Worth; there was also a very fashionable French couturier in those days named Pinguat,
from whom I remember she received a marvellous bot-
tle-green dress; the skirt was of velvet and the basque
of striped green satin with little pink flowers on the
stripes. Over this was a velvet affair which they called
a "visite," worn to afternoon teas—which were events
which filled the winter afternoons of all the women
in society.

Although my father usually liked my mother's
clothes, her "costume," we knew when they missed fire
by a certain derogatory inflection in the word which
he pronounced "caustume." When this green sym-
phony was upon her and she was awaiting his ap-
proval, the glint in his eye presaged his refusal to be
won by it:

"That dress, my dear Lucy, looks like a bedspread!"

And I had thought it perfectly beautiful.

Whenever word came that gowns were being sent
from Paris by a certain boat and would arrive at such
a date in New York, someone from the office always
went down to the Customs to pay the duty and bring
them up to the house. So when a purple velvet costume
arrived one day and the man said there had been no
duty to pay, my mother who was most circumspect in
such matters, sent him back to inquire why it should
have come in duty free.

He came back beaming; "Church vestments, Mrs.

Drexel. When they saw it was purple they said there was no duty."

Mrs. Bradley Martin told me one time that this ecclesiastical free list had been the reason why she had no duty to pay on some house linen which was embroidered with her father's initials: I.H.S. (Isaac H. Sherman); they entered the country as "altar cloths."

When Mrs. Astor refused to pay an unjust duty on her gowns from Paris—the six or eight which she had ordered as usual for her season—they were sold by the Customs with much publicity and a music hall singer managed to make quite a hit with an act in which she suddenly paused and said—or sang—"Oh, those Astor dresses!" as though she had one of them herself. If she had it was a beautiful dress, for Mrs. Astor made no pretence at economy; her reason for refusing to pay the duty—she had the true bills to show—was that it would have set a precedent of allowing a valuation other than the real one and a lead for others to follow.

One time as she got off the boat the customs man asked: "As you stand, Mrs. Astor, do you think you are wearing more than the law allows?" (Meaning the value allowed.)

"If I am," she replied, goodnaturedly, *"you* won't like it and if I'm not *Mr. Anthony Comstock* won't like it."

She was not like Mrs. Morgan who surprised my mother by wearing the same dress to a dinner at our house two years in succession:

"I make a point of doing it," she explained, "so that people won't think I am extravagant."

It was the same sort of conservatism as that which a cape of my mother's always seemed to me to express: a cape of heavy black brocaded material which looked almost sombre until you discovered that it was lined with a brilliant scarlet.

One evening, having put it on in her room hastily, she found on coming downstairs that it was on wrong side out. What to do? For she believed in that superstition that it brings bad luck to change anything put on wrong side out.

"I'll wear it this way," she said, but my father protested and she admitted that it was "too *voyant*," to use her favorite expression. So she turned it but worried all the evening over the inevitable bad luck.

"Yet it really was too *voyant!*" she kept saying.

In those days women did not think that they could have different furs every winter. I recall my mother having a chinchilla coat slightly altered by having the flare, which had been fashionable, sewed down as pleats which had come into fashion. And I remember that she carried her sealskin bag several years.

Women were certainly more conscious of their clothes when they wore more of them over stiff corsets and bustles and wiped up the sidewalks with their "balayeuse" than they do today; it used to seem to me that they were quite nervous in church for fear that their dresses would get mussed. At any rate church was one of the favorite places for showing off clothes, although the opera had a rarer and more official standing as a show room. Yet I knew only one woman who went to the extreme of exhibiting her gowns and jewels by having a chair for her opera box built especially high so that more of her magnificent torso could be seen.

She was the first woman, my mother said, to have her opera glasses fixed to a long handle to hold like a lorgnon; her ample and exuberant figure made this almost imperative, for in a tight waist it was quite impossible for her to get her plump arm up to the usual opera glass level.

Another great place for the presentation of costumes was the Horse Show. At Newport, as in New York, it lasted a week and it was a matter of strict form to wear a different costume at each performance—and not to miss *any* of the events. In New York the boxes were numbered on the program so that those who came could know who was who. The "Four Hundred" were not unwilling, either, to be stared at, although they might not always have been pleased with the comments. I overheard a woman below our box saying to her escort: "Think what these women can have to eat if they want it!"

And his disdainful reply: "Probably crackers and vinegar so as to take off fat."

But the desire to show off belongs to no one set of

people. When I was a child we had a cook who enjoyed immensely what she believed to be the impression she made on a Sunday afternoon when she emerged by way of the basement steps from our house on Madison Avenue. She always waited until the street was clear before she came up; it was evident that she did not want anyone to think she belonged to the basement part of the house. She wore a bright purple dress and a purple bonnet, a Paisley shawl and a mink muff!

She walked slowly down the avenue with a majestic air which was due to entire self-satisfaction. When summer came and she could no longer carry the muff, she put one hand firmly upon her solar plexus and carried the other stiffly by her side.

Anne Quinn lingered in my memory because of a song which used to echo throughout the basement: "I love beauty, I love beauty, I love beauty fairly well."

Years after I discovered I had not heard it aright; what she had been singing was: "Isle of beauty, Isle of beauty, Isle of beauty, fare thee well."

But the Machine Age finally affected clothes; the appropriate costume came in when the bicycle had been invented. Mrs. Belmont used to boast that she was one of the first women to wear bloomers when she mounted her wheel. They were voluminous and can hardly be considered the direct ancestor of "shorts" or even of pyjamas. The divided skirts, the habits of women who dared to ride cross-saddle, the shorter and shorter skirts on the tennis court—until one day they disappeared entirely—all these fashions did not affect the sumptuous dinner and ballroom gowns; two worlds marched side by side.

And although the cost of the clothes for parade mounted, we did not see anything excessive in the prices asked; we took them as a matter of course. It did, however, seem extravagant of Mrs. Leeds to spend her dress allowance of forty thousand dollars a year and not be satisfied. But in her case it was more the pleasure of buying than of wearing, for we used to ask her why, when she had a dozen costumes for outdoor wear, she never put on anything else except the one or two which had become her favorites. She liked them and she wore them the season throughout, bestowing on her friends gowns which she had not worn once, letting her maids have others which were not *worn* although she may have had them on too often to give to anyone in her circle.

Not that her dresses would be worn without altering by most of those who became their owners, for she was stout. Yet not so stout as a certain woman who took so much material in the making of her gowns that Worth said he had to charge double when she ordered clothes of him. She did not object. I think she was even proud of the vast expanses which she used to have covered, as she said, with "gemanty" (*diamanté*). And when she appeared in the evening with all her jewels on, she seemed to be pushing ahead of her a capacious shelf covered with diamonds.

The day was passing though when anyone could say again of Mabel Gerry who adored lace flounces . . . "Why doesn't she wear her petticoat on the outside?" Or when a cousin of mine could find all the space needed for the embroideries of cupids and musical instruments on her lingerie just as she had designs taken from Boucher's paintings to adorn her table-cloths.

Even what Lady Townley wrote of as "mutton-chop sleeves," meaning "leg-of-mutton," were diminishing until today an evening gown may have none at all.

Pinkie Andrews was much concerned on coming out of the opera that his companion, who had a bad cold, should be so décolleté:

"Oh, but I have on high shoes," she said.

But there have always been wise women who know how to economize without having to broadcast the reason. There was a woman who had three daughters to bring out in New York—and keep out—until they married. Her position allowed her to move in the "best" society but her purse was meagre. At any rate we noticed that the year all three girls were finally launched and would be accepting invitations—which would mean several party dresses for each one—they all appeared in mourning—white evening gowns, black the rest of the time. That allowed them to wear the same dress constantly as a matter of course. The death they mourned was that of a fictitious aunt!

The day is well past when men dress with any idea of being noticed for their clothes. When my father used to go to Saratoga he was conspicuous because he did *not* wear jewelry. And today the well-dressed man would echo Jimmie Cutting's assertion that he made whenever anyone commented on the soberness of his attire: "I want my clothes to be as near as possible to what everyone else is wearing." In time that desire became a principle and he was terribly shocked to find that he had not brought tails when he arrived at a house-party and found that there was a formal dinner on.

He was so relieved when Harry Lehr said: "Don't give it a thought, I'll arrange it."

The smoking jacket which his man had taken to brush came back with two towels pinned on behind.

Yet one of the most effective fancy-dress costumes I have ever seen was one made from two table-cloths and a napkin—and without any cutting having been done; it was worn on a cruise in the South Atlantic by a passenger who had not brought any fancy dress with her. She won the prize.

It was on a South American quay that I saw, during that same voyage, a row of white leather travelling bags, of all sizes, and trunk of the same leather, which called to mind the "luggage" which the world used to carry about without considering it an expression of the de luxe crafts. I stood there in admiration before that

carefully made assortment of containers for clothes and
hats, for golf sticks and all the rest of the modern
equipment, which is at home on any continent, although usually bearing a Paris or London maker's
name whose world fame is assured. How different
from the trunks and bags which we used to see piled
up on the pier or being thrown into the baggage car
of the train for Saratoga! Now smart baggage is of a
chosen color and texture throughout.

Luxury used to be of the home; today it is transferred to the steamer,—a "blue ribbon" one if possible,
or to the auto or to some rainbow "arrow" which hur-
tles through from Constantinople to London. Travelling used to be a more or less painful displacement, the
mind being fixed upon the goal as the end of such
miseries as sea-sickness, cinders in the eye, or thirst.

Taking the train for Saratoga was a big event but it
had nothing of the travel poster about it. You wore
a travelling dress which shed the dust—sometimes grey
alpaca because black was too sombre for the young.
The dressmaker found even that "too sad" for my
doll's dress and trimmed it with two rows of red braid.
Then there were the inevitable linen "dusters" which
got completely wrinkled in the first hour of wear. And
my mother wore veils thick enough to keep out the air
and to keep the hair in order. What an odd smell they
had, those green veils.

There were no dining cars on that line when we
first used to go to the "Queen of Spas," so we had our

lunch in a basket with two handles: hard boiled eggs and the salt in small squares of paper, Larrabee's biscuits and fruit; you threw all the wrapping papers out of the window when you had finished. That lunch-basket did not have the dignity of the usual English "tea-basket" that I was to know later. I remember when Consuelo Vanderbilt became the Duchess of Marlborough an Englishwoman said to her, as though it were a special privilege, "A duchess can have a basket."

Even further back—it was my mother who gave me the picture—there was the little side-wheeler which carried her and her sister across the Delaware from Tacony to Burlington where they went to school; and the custom of having a buggy or gig meet you and carry you home from the wharf acquired the dignified appellation of "gigmanity." The house that she lived in as a child could be seen from the railroad till a few years ago—unchanged—but nothing which passed it on wheels, nothing which floats upon the river now, looks at all the same as in those days.

Yet even the houses become less substantial in this world of contrast when you consider them from the air; they might be anthills for all the dignity which looking down on them permits. We are in a revolution which is so visible that no one is taking the slightest notice of it. . . .

On the steamer crossing the Atlantic in the old days you had time to watch the waves in the wake of the boat; today the ship goes so fast that it would give you vertigo even if the multiple social duties entailed by the presence of the bar, of the cinema, the deck sports, and dancing, left you any desire to see the vasty deep. If a steamer was sighted *then* it was an event. Today it is only the S O S which can rouse the passengers from their amusements. No steamer in sight but invisible danger towards which the Captain must turn to give aid!

Today few ships come into port without having had the beginnings of fires on board because someone let a cigarette fall carelessly.

"We say nothing of such fires," said the Captain of a great Transatlantic liner to me, "but we are on the watch for them from the moment we sail. That is why you see so many more stewards in proportion to the passengers than you used to."

And the clothes! Today they are bought from the most fashionable couturiers just for the chance to show them on board ship; in the old days you wore old clothes on board—my father always wore flannel shirts and a Scotch cap—and kept your good clothes "for going ashore." Steamer chairs were the exception, benches fastened to the decks did very well for the majority of the voyagers.

There are so many contrasts—and all of them seem so significant as though they ought to be interpreted by some historian as a moral lesson.

In New York it is not only the tall buildings which

make me aghast, it is also the elevators in them. Over here in France we are still in the primitive stage of elevators; they are a human sort of carrier whose tops are usually open, so that you could crawl out of them if they should get stuck between two floors. But in America the elevator is a tight piece of machinery in the form of a closed box which slides at lightning speed up and down—how many stories?

At the Ritz Hotel in New York I wanted to go down to the room of a friend on the next floor below to have dinner. As I was wearing a negligee I did not care to descend in the elevator with the superb guests going down or out to dine. So I called the chambermaid and asked—a little surprised that I had not yet seen them—where the stairs were.

"There aren't any," she said blandly.

That gave me a peculiar shock. I felt that I was not only cut off from the friend one story down but from the whole outer world. Stairs had never seemed so important to me before, so absolutely essential. I was so startled that I showed it. And the girl before me suddenly took interest in my wish for stairs.

"There *is* the fire-escape," she suggested, "which we servants use. It is *inside*."

I used it. And I measured how many flights I would have to go down in case of fire—it was not very comforting but it could save one's life—the walls were rough brick, the stone steps open.

It was in another hotel, when I was waiting on the

twelfth floor for the elevator, that I saw a woman put out her cigarette and look hopefully about for an ash-tray.

"Ah!" she said triumphantly as she stuck it in the slit of the letter shaft.

"Yes, indeed!" said the clerk at the desk, "the letters are very often burnt up when they get down here; we have to sweep their ashes out of the box."

Sometimes I begin to believe that the "modern" artists are inspired after all, that their wild view of people and *nature morte* may be the way we really look. Our perspective has changed and we might as well admit it as frankly as that artist whom I caught painting in the garden of an old château where we were both week-ending.

Although he was looking intently at a distant garden wall, I saw nothing on his canvas which resembled it, yet he seemed quite happy, not at all as though he were trying to do something impossible.

Finally I asked him what he was doing.

"I am deforming the perspective," he said genially, and pointed out with perfect *sang-froid* that although the garden wall and walks really ran towards a vanishing point—as I had been told in my youth—and although things did apparently get smaller as they receded along those walks, he was getting immense pleasure out of painting the flowers in the background as big as trees and the tree in the foreground as small as a tiny rose-bush.

It was quite a lesson—not that he was at all original in doing it this way. . . . Hogarth drew a man at a window in the foreground who, with his candle, was lighting the pipe of a man on a distant mountain. But Hogarth never pretended to be serious even though you could, if you wanted to, take the picture for an allegory.

If, however, artists keep on distorting the world about them, it may make what we see seem less monstrous as the transformations go on and on under the spell of the age we live in.

Brown Brothers, photo.

THE CLIFFS, NEWPORT

CHAPTER XIX

SUPERSTITIONS

SUPERSTITIONS, HOWEVER, DO NOT CHANGE; THEY STAY steady in their power over our minds and we had better call our traditions by that word if we want to preserve them. I have rarely known anyone who was not superstitious. Yet I have told a great many people superstitions which they had never heard of and which—I saw by the look in their eyes—they were going to accept at once as gospel truth—a new thing to be afraid of and, so, very important.

When I made my first visit to a Scotch castle I was told not to mention any queer sound or sight I might experience. "There is always a ghost of some sort and it is usually connected with an ancient scandal or tragedy which the host does not care to tell you even to explain what has just frightened you."

So I sealed my lips and began to feel very eerie in any out-of-the-way corner of that castle—and most of the corners seemed to be out-of-the-way and full of mystery. But—nothing happened. It was only much later when I was visiting some Americans who had rented a famous old castle for the season that I had my "experience."

The splendid room which had been given me was off a hall hung with family portraits—very Scotch in their uniforms and kilts—for they were all portraits of men of the family. I had to run the gauntlet of their fixed regards every time I came to my room or left it, but I did not give a thought to any of them except a rather badly painted picture of a man of the eighteenth century as I could judge by his uniform.

The first time my eye caught his I shuddered, and after that took care not to look his way as I hurried by. But it was hard to avoid that gaze of his because he hung directly above these steps which I had to use to reach my bathroom. Worse than that I *felt* him looking at my back when I went down these steps and to avoid that I found myself going down sideways.

Yet I was ashamed to say anything about such an absurd sensation and used to gain my room by going through the adjoining one when its occupant was not in it. I hurried to my bath in the morning my maid in my room—I was ashamed to tell her of my feelings—and, once downstairs, I would stay all day until time to dress for dinner, when I would scurry along that corridor as though I were pursued.

Familiarity did not diminish the feeling and at last I confided to my maid that I was "afraid" of that picture and to find out, if she could, from some of the servants who this man was—but without telling why she wanted to know. And then I told her she would have to be with me when I passed that picture or I should have to leave the castle on some pretext or other.

There were several servants who had stayed on when the Earl rented the castle to my friends—two or three housemaids.

"Oh, that mon!" said one of them, "why he was the lord of the castle who killed the drummer-boy. The drum is up there in the fifth tower."

The drummer-boy had come from those who were besieging the castle and he carried a white flag. This "lord of the castle" had listened to his message and then, killing him, had hung his body out of the tower window where it could be recognized by those who had sent him.

No wonder that I had not wanted those eyes on my back! But since I had learned that there had been good reason for my feeling as I did, I confided to my American hostess what the chambermaid had said.

"And the Earl told us when he gave us the keys that he was giving us everything *but* a ghost," she said.

I heard afterwards that one guest of the Earl and Countess who had had my room and who had not been told what the etiquette was in a Scotch castle, had gone to lunch one day and asked:

"Do you keep a drummer-boy?"

To her amazement her hostess grew white as death. For it was a superstition in the family that whenever the lord of the castle was going to die, that little drum, which was stuck into the wall of the tower—and which no one dared to take down—could be heard drumming.

Two days later the news came that the Earl of ——
had been killed at Spion Kop in South Africa!

Knowing the story of the man who put to death the
youthful messenger bearing a white flag did not lessen
my fear. "How can I pass that picture?" I would ask
myself whenever I opened my door in the morning, or
when it was time to regain my room at night.

I knew then how Mrs. Belmont had felt about a certain Pre-Raphaelite picture she had owned which she
insisted made weird sounds no matter where she placed
it. She finally gave it away to her daughter who hung
it where the sounds could not be heard—if they kept
on.

Many people, I discover, have never heard that it
brings very bad luck to give away a wedding dress for
someone else to wear.

Yet that superstition was one of the first I learned,
because my mother, not knowing it, had given her un-
used wedding dress and veil to a friend. The friend
died soon after the wedding.

That my mother should have the dress and veil to
give away was the direct consequence of Lincoln's
death. He had been shot on April fourteenth and died
the next day. My mother and father were to be married on the eighteenth. As the whole country was in
deep mourning there must be no lace veil and long-
trained white dress.

So my mother had another dress made and she trimmed herself a bonnet with white violets—which must have made her look prettier than ever. And she made a gift of what she had not been able to wear to a friend who was to be married some time later. The death which followed made a great impression upon her—and upon me when I heard of it.

The story of Mrs. Belmont's wedding dress confirmed the superstitition, for it too carried a heavy load of misfortune. She had ordered it from Worth's, but fearing that it would arrive too late for her wedding, she had had another made in New York. When the exquisite Worth dress came she gave it at once to a friend—whose engagement had just been announced. Shortly after she heard that the engagement had been broken.

This woman, knowing she would never wear the dress, gave it to a friend of hers. That time the dress was worn but the marriage soon proved unhappy. A third time the dress was given and it was worn, but the wearer died in child-birth and was buried in it!

There may be some basis for a strong personal superstition, either in the superstition or in the one who believes it, but there is not much need of looking for a basis if you believe in fortunetellers. Once you have heard that one of So-and-So's predictions came true, it is hard not to accept all of them as foretelling the inevitable. Mrs. Fish never doubted the word of any clairvoyant and she had a passion for consulting them.

Just as surely as you had to visit hospitals with Mrs. Oelrichs you had to visit clairvoyants with Mrs. Fish.

One day when I could not, or would not, go to see a famous person she had heard of and wanted to consult, Harry Lehr went with her. We were to meet at the train late in the afternoon, and we did. We had seats in the parlor-car and our bags and umbrellas were put in place; I seated myself and both of them disappeared.

Since they were always going through trains before we started, I did not miss them until we had pulled out of the station. Even then I expected to see them appear—but not a sign of them! So I decided that they had been left behind.

No indeed! As we came into the station at Garrisons where we were to get off the train, there they were, looking a little sheepish. They had been riding, they said, in the day-coach. A long time afterwards Mrs. Fish told me why: She had persuaded Harry Lehr to have his fortune told. And the clairvoyant had said that I was to die very soon in a railway accident—that he was to be a widower. As train accidents were always possible and as my death was quite inevitable they had decided it would be safer for them to be as far away as possible!

They had—quite literally—left me to my fate!

But that prediction never disturbed me for I, for my part, had been told I was to be a widow. And it is

human nature to believe the clairvoyant *you* have consulted and not the other.

A dream I had made a deep impression on me once.

It was during the War; we were in New York and
six of us were to sail together on the *Lusitania*. Mrs.
Leeds was of the party and as she had left with her
"lovely stewardess," her special steamer blankets, her
lace pillows, her perfumes, soaps, and all the rest of
the things she would want for her return trip, her suite
was ready for her—a suite which cost thousands of dollars for each voyage.

Like everyone else I had heard the rumors that the
Lusitania was marked for destruction and read the
German announcements of its destruction every day.
The New York *Herald* had a terrifying cartoon of the
danger realized. That cartoon impressed me tre-
mendously.

At the hotel Mrs. Leeds had her rooms up on the
twelfth floor; ours were lower down. And Count von
Bernsdorf, the German ambassador, had the suite next
to ours. I used to wonder whether he did not have
something to do with the notes I found several times
pinned to my door, saying: "Do not sail on the *Lusitania!*" His ancestor had been called, by Frederick the
Great, "the oracle of Denmark."

I had long ago reserved a large suite but without
paying for it, so that I could change my mind. However, when the steamship offices sent word they could

not hold it longer if I did not pay—I paid, and from that moment my fear increased. Whenever we dined at the Goelets or the Vanderbilts my anxiety about the voyage was found very amusing.

"We certainly envy you the chance to sail on the *Lusitania!*" said Mrs. Vanderbilt.

And Anthony Drexel would say—for he was to be one of the six in our party—"Think how big it is! Nothing can hurt a boat as big as that!"

"The bigger it is," I would answer, "the better mark for the enemy."

"But think of its speed!" he'd say.

My answer to that was: "That would only make death come the swifter!"

Then he would point out that they had a second crow's nest, a very high one. My reply was that only allowed the lookout to see the enemy further away but could not prevent danger. He talked, too, of there being mine-sweepers with the ship—two of them. This, however, did not prove to be the case.

As they were all insistent, to please them I gave in. And then, the night of the thirteenth—we were to sail on the fifteenth—I dreamed that I was in the sea and that I was struggling to keep afloat. There were hundreds of people in the water with me, and they were all trying to keep from drowning. There seemed no hope of being rescued—no hope at all!

When I wakened it was daylight; I didn't wait to dress; I put on a negligee and, after telephoning her maid to waken her, I went up to Mrs. Leeds' room. Trembling from head to foot I told her the dream and said: "If there is another ship sailing tomorrow I'll take it with you, but I will *not* go on the *Lusitania*."

All Mrs. Leeds could think of, however, was the magnificent ship, with its correct British personnel and seamen, her pillows and her blankets and the little pink shaded lamp she always had to have waiting for her in the suite she had engaged, but when she saw I was determined, she suggested that we look in the paper.

The *New York* was sailing. We telephoned for the two suites de luxe and several extra rooms, and I had all my baggage unmarked before I stopped to take breath, so that there would be no excuse for its being sent to the *Lusitania* by "mistake." The American Line sent up a representative with our tickets and labels and relabelled for the *New York*.

We were to go on board the next morning, but to reassure myself until then I went upstairs after the theater that night again to see whether they had changed the tags on Mrs. Leeds' baggage. There in the hall, before her rooms, was a man with a revolver. He was walking back and forth in front of the long row of baskets and bags and packages some of which had been sent her as "bon voyage" gifts; what a line of them! When I appeared, he came forward and stopped me:

"What do you want?" he asked.

"I want to see if the tags on these things are for the *New York*."

He came between me and the baskets. Very quickly indeed I told him who I was. Fortunately he knew my name and fortunately he believed me. He was there, he said, to protect this baggage.

The tags were for the *New York*, but I did not sleep too well that last night since it was still my one will against all the others. The next morning there was one of those terrible New York blizzards and there was no question in this snow and fog of sailing at nine o'clock as planned. Most unfortunately this delay permitted the discussion to start all over again!

"Think of the two refrigerators of special delicacies I had sent to the *Lusitania*," said Mrs. Leeds.

It was better, according to my way of thinking, to lose those two refrigerators of game and fruit than to be food for the fishes.

At last we boarded the *New York*, which was not far from the dock where the *Lusitania* herself was waiting for the storm to let up. Imagine my dismay when I heard that that ship had sent someone over to talk to Mrs. Leeds and to point out that her rooms and the other suites—for we had paid for them all—were in readiness for us. They even appealed to her sympathy.

"Think what an effect it will have on our reputation when the papers learn you would not sail with us."

I wondered at her holding out.

"And do you call *this* a suite de luxe?" asked Mrs.

Leeds plaintively, after the *Lusitania* man had gone.
"I didn't call it anything," I said. "It was the man
over the 'phone who said it was de luxe."

Of course there was no comparison with her usual
suite; and I did not particularly like mine either. But
I had my things unpacked very quickly and everything
put into place so that if the others should change their
mind I, at least, would remain where I was.

I admit that up to the last minute I was terribly
afraid that those refrigerators and lace pillows and
down quilts were going to pull them out of the *New
York* and over to the *Lusitania*.

"The rest of you can do what you want to," I said.
"*I* shall stay on this ship."

Anthony Drexel had told us, when we first talked of
the *New York*, that after all it was a fine boat—he had
crossed on her on her first voyage; but he had been
surprised to see that instead of our going up the gang-
plank when we got to the pier, we went *down!* It gave
him quite a shock—it seemed to have shrunk.

It seemed queer when, at five o'clock and we had
finally left our pier, to pass under the very stern of the
Lusitania and look *up* at it, from *our one deck!* It
felt as though we were in a little steamer of the pre-
historic variety.

The *Lusitania* was of enormous bulk, but it had
had its name filled in and painted black; its funnels
too were black. The ship was camouflaged. *And it was
carrying the Irish flag!*

I heard afterwards that on a former voyage, when going through the English Channel where the mines were, it had hoisted the Stars and Stripes. But Bernsdorf had gone at once to the President, who had summoned the officials of the Cunard Line; they explained that they had run up that flag because "there were Americans on board."

The *New York* sailed out into the night as brightly lighted as a birthday cake—so that the stars and stripes painted from stem to stern could be seen by any and all Germans.

Such precautions were consoling. I began to feel pride in my stubbornness. Nothing was going to happen to us. I saw the *Lusitania* in the shadow of black funnels whenever I thought of her. But I did not like to think of her; it brought back my dream too vividly. . . .

When we got to Liverpool, there ahead of us was the *Lusitania*, already docked. And everyone had their laugh at my expense. My pride finally went down under their amusement; I felt very small.

But they did not laugh later when they heard that before the end of the next voyage the *Lusitania* had been sunk.

And who knows whether it was not intended to send it to the bottom on the voyage for which we were booked?

Being blessed—or cursed—with the lack of imagination that would induce me to cross bridges before I come to them I am frequently in the midst of danger before I have the slightest inkling of it. . . .

On this occasion had there been any way to get out I would not have hesitated an instant, but the aisle between the seats of the auto-car had been filled with *strapontins,* upon which were seated bulky tourists. We were in a trap! And we had forty-five kilometers to go!

"If we ever get up," I said to my sister, "we'll go back on foot!"

Looking from the window on my side, I could see no margin of a road—nothing but a precipice. And looking across the car I could see that we were near the wall of rock! Yet I had laughed merrily when my maid had balked at going because they had asked her before starting to write down the name of the person "to be informed in case of accident."

I decided—all too late—that she had been very wise.

When my father and mother had come to the monastery on the St. Bernard Pass, they had had to ride mules; there was a cold wind and they were far from having what my mother loved to call "creature comforts"—such as the warm air of a train compartment. But they had not been in any danger of rolling off into space. How I longed to be seated on the bony backs of those most sure-footed of animals which had served my parents. My terror kept on increasing as we mounted higher and higher. Nothing happened. We arrived.

But what an anti-climax! There, ahead of us, was a Cook's Tour. It was like coming into a well-populated village instead of to a stern monastery in one of the world's lonely places.

We did not like the idea of going to the "cook's" dining-room with this crowd and my sister, who had been up here before, led me to the monks' refectory, where distressed travellers were formerly served and allowed to make their "offering" if they felt so inclined.

To our disgust one of the tourists kept his gaze upon us—and followed. There we were. He did not follow our example when it came to making the "offering"!

It was a strange place to eat in, the windows nothing but small spaces in the wall, with double glass to keep out the fearful snow and cold. And from the odor it was evident that the dogs and donkeys were directly beneath in their stables.

"You must see the piano!" said my sister and we went into the salon where it was, a tiny instrument since it too had had to come up on mule-back. For it was the gift of Edward VII who, after a visit here had asked the monks what they wanted most: "A piano!"

But when my sister had seen it the first time, there had been a monk sitting at it, singing songs such as no one would ever expect a St. Bernard monk to know—and in English!

She sat there petrified, listening to what sounded to her like rankest ribaldry. Suddenly he turned to her and asked with noisy good-nature how she had found the coming up. Her answer was frigid.

"And how do you like my costume?"

She was silent.

"I'm wearing *their* costume," he said boisterously, "while my clothes are drying. I've been rescued."

The atmosphere cleared.

The silver candlesticks which my sister had on that trip brought up as souvenirs of my father's and mother's visit, were on the altar. She had carried one tied on behind her saddle; the other behind Miss Roberts', her companion—for they, too, had ridden mules. The candlesticks were still on the altar, the monks wanted to show us their other treasures—all of them marks of interest from those who had come up here.

We climbed a short ladder to a loft above and there, in sharp contrast with the room of plain deal board, was the most magnificent collection of vestments! Napoleon, who passed here in 1800, had given some of them.

And outside, although it was August, were the mountains with the snow still on them—mountains where, the year round, those marvellous dogs search for those who are lost and when they have discovered them and dug them out and given them brandy from their flasks, to climb with what seems like human intelligence, slip their paw through a noose and ring a bell to summon the monks.

One of the dogs had saved forty-four men; the forty-fifth, rousing from delirium and seeing this huge creature covering him had, in sudden terror, shot him.

It was to this place three hundred years after the

St. Bernard of Menthon and the first monks had built the hospice that we had come *in a touring car!*

The rigors of winter here are so terrible that no monk may remain more than five years—and no one can be more than twenty-six years old.

We did not walk down for the simple reason that I was ashamed to let anyone know how frightened I was. But, instead of peering down the precipices, I kept my eyes straight ahead of me. That is the stupid way I have always gone through life.

CHAPTER XX

TRADITIONS

"ONE OF THE FIRST THINGS I FELT IN AMERICA," WRITES
Lady Susan Townley in her *Indiscretions*—"no matter in what social center, was the disadvantages to hostesses of having no traditions to fall back upon. We do
not realize in the dear Old World, until we see in
America, the embarrassment caused by the absence of
it, how entirely we depend upon time-honored custom
for reference and comparison. . . ."

Realizing that, as she did, it is surprising to find how
extremely critical Lady Susan was of our shortcomings
due to no fault of our own—if we accept what she went
on to say. . . .

"In America there is no way of measuring the social
fitness of things. Each hostess is a law unto herself. And
thus it is that feminine rivalries are born, and necessity
arises to outdo one's neighbor—a necessity which be-
trays American hostesses into extravagances often bor-
dering upon and sometimes overstepping the limits of
good taste."

No one can appeal from such judgment, but she was
mistaken about each hostess being a law unto himself.
. . . She did know Miss de Barril. She could not be ex-

pected to know Miss de Barril who seldom appeared at
large functions although she made a majestic figure in
her gowns trimmed with "bugles," or whatever was the
fashionable equivalent, for she loved ornament and
wore it to the interest of her observers; she liked
brooches and chains.

And that was quite natural. We used to call her
"Inca"—she had come from a Spanish-American country. She had brought with her an innate love of formality and a marvellous Gothic handwriting; and out
of those two things she made a career for herself.

We all knew the story of her coming: to visit an
uncle who had been the Minister of Finance of his
country until, becoming rich, he had come to New
York to live. There, believing that his money would
open all portals, he built himself a handsome house
and sent out invitations. But his acquaintances were
few and he spent the remaining years of his life in
that immense and empty house on Madison Square,
cared for by his young and Spanish-looking niece
who loved the grandeur of the big house.

Family fortune failing as suddenly as it began, Maria
de Barril had to make her living. It was Ward Mc-
Allister, I think, who took her to see Mrs. Astor—and
her ability to write invitation lists with a perfect understanding of the distinctions to be made between the
names which were upon them—did the rest. She addressed the envelopes in that perfect handwriting of
hers and what was more important for her success she

Brown Brothers, photo.

COACHING PARADE IN NEW YORK CITY

was discretion itself while willing to be helpful to all
those who used her services.

For her usefulness to Mrs. Astor opened all doors to
her, and all the women who wanted to be sure they
were not making any blunder which might offend the
acknowledged leader of the "Four Hundred" called
upon Miss de Barril to help them with *their* lists of
invitations. Indeed her handwriting upon an envelope
was a sign that the person giving the party was within
the pale. For she herself drew the line where her services stopped.

Little by little she became a sort of social day-book;
she was consulted to find if the evening chosen had
been taken by any other hostess. Then she came to be
such an institution all by herself that her "clients"
would simply put their tentative lists in her hands and
she would order the cards engraved, see that they were
sent out, and very often help in the arrangements for
the entertainment. It was she who filed all the accept-
ances and saw that there were no blunders either in
including the wrong people or leaving out the right
ones, through oversight.

Every year she went to Newport and had the same
room in the same boarding-house, from which then
issued those hundreds and hundreds of invitations
which made the season's gaicty. In her little parlor
there was a table covered with a lace "spread" on which
was the oddest assortment of hearts I have ever seen—
in silver and gilt, in glass and faïence and painted wood

—boxes and trays. Everyone gave her a "heart"; they were her hobby.

Perhaps the heart stood for confidence; certainly she gained and held those of her clients who, although they only paid two cents apiece for the addressing of each envelope and I do not know how little for filling in the engraved cards, began to call upon her to receive society reporters.

If the advance news of a social affair was needed, off to Miss de Barril went the reporter, who would return with the description of costumes to be worn, the number of guests invited, the form of entertainment, and it could all be written before the party. This rôle of intermediary must have helped support her but she never abused her position. And no amount of luxury ever surprised her; the invariable comment was . . . "My uncle used to have that in his house. . . ."

She was a sort of social clearing-house. And I am certain that as long as she lived to fulfil her destiny there were not many hostesses who were a law to themselves.

Mrs. Blank and her mother, Mrs. X, were said to spend every morning cutting down the lists they made of those whom they considered eligible for invitation to their parties—whereat as someone said, only the coachmen and chauffeurs were warm and comfortable in the sort of lunch-wagon which she provided for them outside the house on winter ball-nights, in New

York. A long-suffering *invité* once remarked that two
of the pearls in Mrs. X's necklace had not been able
to resist the cold. She did not seem to notice, however,
and continued to wear these two dead pearls whenever
she presided over a party.

Ned Randolph decided one evening that he must
do something to break the monotony of the conversation as he stood talking with Mrs. X in that formal
way she had adopted years before and never altered.
She gave him the opening. . . .

"Who is that pretty woman over there?" she asked
in her detached way.

"She is pretty, isn't she?" he replied. "I've just had
a child by her."

Mrs. X's start of horror before she realized the
lady was his wife, and her frigid displeasure at his
way of announcing it was more than he had hoped for;
he was jubilant all the rest of the evening.

Mrs. B. called all but a very few select persons
"bizarre people." And when the Pembroke-Joneses,
who came under that heading in her eyes, sent out invitations for a large party she took the occasion, after
carefully finding out what evening it was to be, to
send out invitations for one of her own. But those who
had accepted the invitation of the "bizarre people" did
not decide to give up the bigger party to accept; and
she had to call her party off. A splendid dinner of three
hundred followed by a ball of the Pembroke-Jones,
one harassed couple, the M——s, who could not bear

to refuse an invitation of dinner and bridge at Mrs. B's exclusive villa, thought out what seemed a clever compromise: the husband called up Mrs. Jones on the day of the dinner.

"Poor little Gladys is *so* ill, but she wants me to come just the same—I have done everything I can to make her comfortable. . . ."

Mrs. Jones told him to come alone and that she would come over in the morning to see Gladys.

Meanwhile Gladys went to the bridge-party at Mrs. B's and swore everyone to secrecy; no one was ever to mention her being here when she was supposed to be in bed—everyone swore except the attaché of the German Embassy, who had just arrived from Washington and no one thought of his knowing the Jones'.

He arrived late at the Pembroke-Jones dance and to excuse himself to the hostess, he said:

"You must forgif me but I wass held at Mrs. M——'s bridge table so long—I could not get avay."

Mrs. Jones stared at him blankly,—and the poor young diplomat felt that his excuse was being taken rather badly. What he thought when he saw Mr. M—— dancing I do not know, and what were Sadie Jones' feelings!

Few of us, for example, would ever mistake a perfect English butler for one of the invited guests and yet, there was "Silent Smith" coming down in the elevator with a taciturn and distinguished individual at the close of his party in the Waldorf-Astoria—where

the favors for just one figure of the cotillion cost nine
thousand dollars. He put out his hand genially. . . .

"It has been a pleasant evening, hasn't it?"

"Quite," said Morton with distant politeness.

He was Mrs. Fish's butler who had been loaned to
Mr. Smith for the occasion.

But Morton was unique; the only other servant that
I have ever known with as much *sang-froid* was the
coachman of my cousin Mrs. Van Renssalaer. He was
never known to acknowledge any reproof except with
a bow—and then he kept on as before. She was a bride
and felt that her dignity as well as her authority were
at stake, so she finally mustered courage to discharge
him.

To make it perfectly plain she sent for him when
she was on the veranda and told him he must leave, at
once. He bowed.

Two hours later she ordered her victoria, expecting
his late subordinate to drive around to the door. But
there was the object of her ire, immovable, on the box.
She got into the carriage. He stayed on years longer
and proved an invaluable man.

There was among us another famous coachman—one
employed by Mrs. Belle Neilson; he did not at all dis-
claim the flattering rumor that he was the illegitimate
son of a well-known man, from whom, said gossip, he
had inherited both his love of horses and his "style."

The standard set by the men who loved and owned
horses, by those whose stables were known the world

over, gave the coachman a place of distinction which no chauffeur today can ever occupy.

Alfred Vanderbilt was the last great promoter of coaching. He kept it up long after it seemed destined by the turn of the age to go out of fashion; twice a week for years he drove out to Westchester. But as he found that inviting people involved a good deal of uncertainty—not putting on his invitations as Colonel Jay used to do: "Weather permitting," and as he could not be sure that those he invited really wanted to drive with him, he originated the idea of letting them pay for it—as a privilege!

And the highest price demanded was for the box-seat next himself of course. Later he carried out this same practice in England, much to the scandal of some conservative persons, but he found it worth while. For he loved his horses passionately; he had relays waiting for him in the fine harness which was his pride. Dapple greys were his favorites.

In those days we would have been startled, however, to hear a chef say that he had to leave a certain house where he was employed because he could not drive a car, and yet only a few years ago a former cook of mine told me that, as a sign that his day was passing. The château where he had been engaged was in the country at some distance from the market—he was expected to go there in an auto and bring home his provisions.

It is in just such details, of which we take little account usually, that the changing period we are in is writing itself down. On the other hand tradition holds its own when there is enough self-interest to bolster it up. When Alfred Vanderbilt took back home a French chef he had lured away from a famous Paris restaurant, he laid down the rule that the man was not to ask or take commissions in the accepted traditional fashion on whatever he bought for the table, or for the kitchen. He paid him what was an enormous salary just to be sure that there should be none of what he called "chicanery."

Everything went very well for awhile and then he began to have tough chickens served and green fruit— nothing was quite right. He went to the grocer and butcher who had always served him, to complain.

"We are sorry, Mr. Vanderbilt," said the grocer, "but we are not supplying your table any more. Your cook asked such high commissions that we couldn't afford to deal with him."

Eliot Gregory was a prophet as well as a genial critic of the society into which he had been born. I used to meet him at balls and dinners and admire his distinction, which he firmly believed could be acquired by anyone who was willing to study the rules, the habits and customs of European social circles, where manners have become second nature.

What would he have thought of the wife of a well-known American diplomat who on being presented to the Pope, said:

"I am so glad to meet Your Holiness; I knew the late Pope, your father."

Or of that other American woman sitting with the wives of European diplomats on the little folding stools until Royalty should arrive, and who, instead of rising then and letting the stool be taken from her, kept her seat and apologized to the Royal Personage who approached, saying:

"Your Majesty must excuse my not rising but my corns hurt so!"

It is quite evident that we have no training school for those to whom we trust our national prestige and while it is very amusing and keeps us in a sort of Mark Twain attitude towards a fancied King Arthur's court, who can say that we do not hurt sometimes more than prestige by such absence of the abc's of the protocol.

I heard years ago an American ambassador who felt he had not been much of a social success say that the next time he came to Europe to occupy a place of honor he would have a love affair with a French duchess—or her courtly equal wherever he might be. He made the mistake of thinking that it was his puritanical soul which had made him so awkward; it was an utter lack of training for his position.

Yet no one ever really looked down on Miss Leary who had been made a countess by the Vatican; that was because she had such an immensely good heart and put so much of it into everything she did. She was part

Brown Brothers, photo.

MR. AND MRS. ALFRED VANDERBILT, MISS GLADYS VANDERBILT AND
MISS NATALIE KNOWLTON

of my New York pageant, first in the house at 3 Fifth
Avenue and then uptown where she had a marble
façade with gilt lines about the windows, a gilded iron-
grill and pearl-lights in a coronet above her front door
—to be lit up at night.

Miss Leary's dinners were odd. When Harry Lehr
asked why this happened, she said:

"Well, I work to a certain point and then I let nature take its way. . . ."

In other words, she did not have a Miss de Barril to
help her, and the intricacies of invitation and response
wearied her soul. So her table was sometimes rather
mixed. And what a dinner!

"This is not a dinner," said one of her guests when
he saw another and another course being served after
Roman Punch which he took for an ice, "It is a
festival."

The impression was strengthened by the delight
which Miss Leary took in tying bows on anything
which would permit it—fruit baskets and chandeliers,
clocks and candlesticks. The favorite color was red.

"No one can say this table lacks a woman's touch,"
said a guest.

As Miss Leary liked a big dinner party and as her
dining-room in the house at Newport could not seat
everyone, she just let her table run on through two
drawing-rooms, turn at right angles to itself and come
to a stop somewhere on the back piazza. As the door-
way allowed just enough space for the table, the two

guests on either side had to peek at each other in front of the lattice and it left no room for the waiters, there had to be three divisions of them: one for each drawing-room and one for the piazza. I remember that one of the Roche boys dived under the table one evening and came up on the other side.

It was all very gay and the lack of formality gave it its place. Miss Leary herself looked like Joseph Jefferson; she wore a red wig, usually with a white bow or a diamond star in it; her inevitable white dress was high in the back with a square décolleté in front, a white jeweled band about her throat and half sleeves.

The tables had to be dismounted quickly once the luncheon or dinner was over and the carpet was then swept more or less in the sight of the guests. Tessie Oelrichs once seized a carpet-sweeper and had the sort of time she enjoyed with it. . . .

"But she has forgotten to put a bow on it," she called out as she slid it over the parlor carpet.

Another time, after a dinner, Mrs. Oelrichs and I sat down on a sumptuous looking seat, which was on a sort of platform covered with red carpet in the garden. We were asked to get up. We had taken the "throne" prepared for the Cardinal who was expected to come out, at any moment, into the garden.

But Newport was like this for contrasts even in the heyday of its fame. . . . A lunch or a dinner at Miss Leary's who had lived there with her brother, Arthur, before his death a great friend of John Jacob Astor;

and then a formal affair at Mrs. Gambril's where everything was correct and the manner more or less hushed. Or a dinner for three hundred at Mrs. Oelrichs', served in just one hour, with everything hot which should be hot and everything cold which was meant to be cold.

There were the luxurious yachts belonging to the New York or Philadelphia Yacht Club whose coming was awaited with pleasure, but there was besides the "Kat Bote Club" for those who loved the water and wanted to be close to it. One of the rules I remember was: "On sighting a lighthouse observations must be taken through a glass." Needless to say that glass was not a field-glass and there were many lighthouses in Newport. The restrictions were such as the catboat would demand, but the rules were more pompous and the uniform more glorious than any connected with yachts. One late summer there was great excitement when the wager was made that the Kat Bote Club could "round the p'int"—which was Point Judith with a much too strong current to be considered safe for any boat so late in the season. Excitement ran high. Bets were taken and the odds were against the possibility of rounding the point.

When the day arrived, everyone in Newport turned out to see what was likely to prove a dangerous undertaking. Excursions came from Narragansett . . . There was a fearful crowd—and intense interest. But where were the boats? Ah! said everyone, as I thought they didn't dare.

At last they appeared! Each one of the six boats mounted on a dray, and pulled by a team of sturdy horses, the captain of each one in full regalia standing proudly by the mast, smiling and bowing.

Nothing had been said about rounding the point in the water and they were living up to their word in rounding it on land!

CHAPTER XXI

NEWPORT "DEAD"

THE "WORLD" WAS GIVING A FULL PAGE TO THE NEWS that Newport was "dead."

"The reason?" it asked. "The chief one is that Newport has become the laughing stock of the whole world." At which point I pause to remark that if that were true, it was only because the *World,* and other papers which loved exaggeration, had come to look at every event upon that little island as worthy of report to a public eager for gossip. "It has been in full glare of publicity so long, its entertainments have been for so long the butt of joke and cartoon, that today the very people who have made Newport what it is, shun it as the devil shuns holy water."

"Half the great houses," the reporter goes on, "will not be opened this summer. The Frederick W. Vanderbilts' place is boarded up and on the market for sale. 'Ochre Court,' Mrs. Goelet's beautiful château is boarded up and I doubt whether she will ever open it again. 'Wakehurst,' scene of James J. Van Alen's beautiful entertainments, is vacant for the summer. Mr. and Mrs. O. H. P. Belmont will not be here at all; their beautiful 'Belcourt' will remain in the hands of a caretaker. For the first time in Newport history Commodore Elbridge T. Gerry and family will stay away. Their sons will make Tuxedo their headquarters. Mr. and Mrs. Cornelius Vanderbilt, Jr., who have a long lease of 'Beaulieu,' William Waldorf Astor's great place on the cliffs, will be abroad for the summer. . . .

"What remains of 'Society' when these six families keep away from Newport for the summer? . . . .

"The tradespeople are in despair. The real estate men have made little or nothing. One family alone whose bills were $20,000 will not be here. Eight thousand dollars' worth of telegrams were filed at Newport monthly ten years ago where now there is an average of three thousand. . . ."

And with a great flourish this lugubrious scribe ends up with the news that the Mackays and the Whitneys would remain down at Long Island and that there would be "five hundred thousand dollars less" spent in Newport that season.

As the Mackays had never been Newport residents up to this time, their absence was not a subtraction. Later Mrs. Whitney added a charming studio on the cliffs at the end of the lawn (between Mrs. Herman Oelrichs' and Cornelius Vanderbilt's "Beaulieu") which allowed her to feel more kindly towards Newport and to spend much time at her lovely villa there; but Mr. Whitney's care for horses would not let him go anywhere where they were not the chief attraction. And Newport only cared for them in smart turn-

outs; even so, the automobile was alongside every carriage now.

This all made Sunday reading for that part of the
public which was interested in the "doings of Society."
Its only shortcoming was that it had so very little truth
in it. Not that it was important to the world to hear
that the George Vanderbilt place was for sale. But the
real news item was that the Leeds were renting it for
that summer. . . . "Rough Point."

We had the house of Mr. Carter of Philadelphia for
the season; his "Quarterfoil" or, as someone facetiously
put it,—"Quart of Oil," on Narragansett Avenue; and
the portrait Boldini had done of me was exhibited
there.

As for Mrs. Goelet's ever opening her lovely "Ochre
Court" again, she did, and gave wonderful parties. Mr.
Van Alen may have been absent; that may have been
one of the seasons he was avoiding "the widows."

Society was a very different affair, I suppose, before
the newspapers began to use it as one of their means of
livelihood and the Society Editor came into being for
the express purpose of "writing up" the activities of
those who gave parties and took vacations.

Ward McAllister always claimed that he fled from
publicity, yet it was in his lifetime that various and
sundry papers began to devote a great deal of space to
the personalities of the men who had made money
through the development of railroads, real estate, and
steel.

If my father, who was a conservative in speech as well as in action, could say picturesquely that one prominent man was a financial tight-rope walker and sit thus in judgment on speculators, I suppose it is not surprising that the men who began to watch every gesture in the business world of the Goulds and the Astors and the Vanderbilts should devote a Sunday page to the amusements of their families.

But I agree with Eliot Gregory. "In this land, where every reason for interesting one class in another seems lacking, that thousands of well-to-do people (half the time not born in this hemisphere), should delightedly devour columns of incorrect information about New York dances and Lenox house-parties, winter cruises, or Newport dinners and balls, strikes the observer as the 'unexpected' in its purest form."

In 1905, there were two full pages in the Hearst papers given to the dinner which Mrs. Astor had rendered spectacular in the society reporter's eyes simply by inviting seventy-nine guests to meet H.R.H. Prince Louis of Battenberg.

How anyone, even a society reporter, could imagine that Mrs. Astor would give a dinner with four hundred covers to visiting royalty, I do not know. But there it was! Sensational in the extreme: the list of the "four hundred" with lines drawn through the names of the 321 who were not invited. The original idea of the writer was that from the night of that dinner there was an inner circle of "79" in the old one of "400."

Brown Brothers, photo.

MRS. JOHN JACOB ASTOR AND HARRY LEHR
The Decorated Auto Parade at Newport, 1902

Then what conjecturings!

"Mr. and Mrs. Senator Chauncey M. Depew left out and Mr. and Mrs. Paul Morton included! Is Mrs. Astor applauding the current revolution in insurance circles? Who are Richard Peters, Dennis Hare and Eliot Gregory that they should dine at Mrs. Astor's with the Prince while the Pembroke-Joneses and half a dozen Iselins and the Kernochans are condemned to frugal repasts at home? . . .

"What a task for Mrs. Astor! Who but an undisputed autocrat could have accomplished it with serene mind, even if it were her own dinner in her own house? That is why the new list of inner circlers is interesting and valuable—because Mrs. Astor made it, and Mrs. Astor is undisputed in her absolute rule!

"Yet it is apparent that the outside public has not been altogether wrong in its estimate of comparative values in the 'Four Hundred.' The triumphant and exceedingly useful Mr. Harry Lehr and his wife were not forgotten. Neither was Miss Natica Rives, the Lanfear Norries, the Oliver H. P. Belmonts, Center Hitchcock and Alfonso de Navarro—all familiar pillars of New York Society standing on solid rock bottom."

And so, as though this were a new diplomatic arrangement, the papers, following the lead of the *American,* began to debate upon the need of this inner circle and to deplore the lack of exclusiveness which allowed four hundred persons to feel that they belonged in the same highly luxurious group.

And years after, Lady Susan Townley writes: "There is something very thrilling in belonging to a 'smart set' which may in one week be reduced from 400 to 79 by the arbitrary wave of a hostess's pen. That happened in New York in November, 1905, on the occasion of Prince Louis of Battenberg's visit, when old Mrs. Astor, the admitted leader of society, thinned out her invitation list to suit the capacity of her dinner-table. The survivors of that drastic cut were known henceforth as 'Mrs. Astor's elect.' Many formerly prominent women thereby suffered social eclipse. . . .

"Imagine the feelings of London society if the Lord Chamberlain suddenly took it into his head to act in so arbitrary a fashion. He would have the whole College of Dodd's peerage, and the united forces of the College of Heralds to face. It would provoke a scene worthy of 'Alice in Wonderland'!"

Yet if one society reporter had not found it worth while to make a big "story" of those dinner invitations, no one would have given the affair much thought except, perhaps, the disappointed people who could not—for perfectly good reasons—be invited.

As soon as the custom of society reporting became general and special articles began to appear there is no doubt that a great many, who pretended to high disdain, really enjoyed seeing their names in print and began to erect a new standard which, I suppose we may say, came under the aegis of "publicity."

There were not many in the "charmed circle" who

would have done what Willy Vanderbilt did to avoid
being annoyed by reporters after his divorce: tear out
the electric bell from his door and leave the wires
dangling so that it gave an effect of sudden and deadly
rage likely to discourage any news-hunter.

Even *Town Topics* could never have had the influence it came to possess if there had not been two
classes of victims for its news-writers—its gossipers:
those who ran with outstretched hand when they saw
the "representative of the press" appear on the horizon,
and the others who turned their backs while the news-
monger took what was held negligently in the open
and trembling hand. Money perhaps was paid to get
good "write-ups" but much more was paid to be let
alone and not to be mentioned, even by innuendo.

There was no approach which was not used. Let a
rich widow like Mrs. Leeds begin to have attention and
the "representative" came up with some utterly false
story of an approaching marriage which he was about
to print. However false it might be, it would serve to
drive away all the suitors between whom she was trying to decide.

Or, it might be that she would be quoted as having
made fun of some one of them, for whom she had the
friendliest feelings. One such article and her salon
would become an arid desert—for men are afraid of
mockery, particularly when they are hovering hopefully about the "world's richest widow."

Woe to the unfortunate man or woman who gave

any money to this or other publications for the privilege of not being mentioned in their columns. From that moment they were considered the regular support of the magazine or paper. Let them refuse to give money the coming year and they would be stigmatized as having given it the year before and then . . .

"That story we heard last year must have been true," their friends would say, who perhaps had never given it any consideration before.

There were tragedies which were the direct result of Society News columns; much gossip without foundation passed under the bridge but occasionally a true comment would cut so deep that the subject of it would see his situation in a new light—and commit suicide!

The humorous aspects were not wanting either and on one occasion a *Town Topics* writer was the hero of the tale: he had been with a crowd of young society girls and their escorts at a luncheon and amidst much laughter had slipped a napkin ring over the fair finger of one of them and announced that she was his wife.

What was his amazement and her horror to learn that this little farce was looked upon by the law as quite as binding as the more serious and conventional ceremony. The getting un-wed was not at all a humorous affair for either one.

The worst sort of stories were those which one's dignity did not allow to be denied, as for instance the gossip which circulated after Mrs. Kingdon's death that her daughter, Mrs. George Gould, had been callous enough to insist on her taking a voyage with her so that she herself would not have to stay at home—and that death had been the result.

Whereas the truth was that Mrs. Kingdon, who was very ill, had been so full of the idea that if she could but get to Davos in Switzerland she might recover and had pleaded so long to go that finally the doctors consented. Mrs. Gould had done everything to safeguard her mother during the ocean voyage; she had a doctor with her and nurses—but Mrs. Kingdon's will did not support the suffering body and she died just after they arrived at the Ritz.

The rooms long engaged, were on the garden, and that night while we sat in the room adjoining the one where Mrs. Kingdon's body lay, we had to listen to the music of a débutante's party which was being given down there—a ball for Fifi Widener.

When I asked Mrs. Gould if we should not ask the party to be called into the hotel itself or else called off, she shook her head . . .

"It would not be fair!" she said.

And we sat on in the dimly lit room and listened to music which suddenly seemed very grim to me.

After all the lights in the hotel were out, the body was carried down the carpeted stairs in utter silence. Another party was over!

Eliot Gregory had the theory that it was because the average American's life was so humdrum that he read avidly the stories—true or false—of those "Whose wealth permits them to break through the iron circle of work and boredom, who do picturesque and delightful things which appeal directly to the imagination; they build a summer residence in six weeks, with furniture and bric-à-brac, on the top of a roadless mountain; they sail in fairylike yachts to summer seas, and marry their daughters to the heirs of ducal houses."

And he goes on to say that there is in the heart of every ambitious American "the secret hope that with luck and good management they too may do these very things, or at least their children will enjoy the fortunes they have gained."

That may be true but I think an even deeper reason is the more superficial pleasure which every one of us has in pageantry wherever we find it—close at hand or in distant countries. Add to that, the universal human curiosity as to how the other half lives—you being yourself "one-half" in your own eyes—and no other explanation is needed for the emphasis which is put on luxury and color wherever it happens to be.

Eliot Gregory was a little too eager, when he wrote his critical articles and his books, to seem serious. We liked that in him but we enjoyed even more his wit, as on that occasion when someone talking of a gay old rake said—either in defending him from more severe charges or as something in his favor:

"He seduces women's minds . . ."

"It's a pity," said Eliot Gregory, "that he doesn't leave them in an interesting condition."

There is little question that Newport has faded somewhat from the world of fashion, fallen from its pinnacle as the most extravagant summer resort in the world. The changes which would come about just with the rising of another generation would explain this decadence. Newport could have no novelty for the sons and daughters of those who had made it famous; they were very likely to be bored with its notoriety and seek other diversions than those which it offered.

But even as early as 1900, Baedeker was becoming conservative about Saratoga and putting Newport ahead—together with Lenox. We used to read: "No more effective picture of the wealth of the United States can be seen anywhere than at Saratoga during July and August though Newport and Lenox show greater refinement of luxury."

That refinement had always belonged in the Newport of the Sheldons and Fearings and Gambrils who had tradition behind them. The Eastlake Period of furniture had left them stone cold; they cherished their solid mahogany in houses built with bricks brought across the ocean on sailing ships. And yet they saw the "period" pendulum swing their way. "Beechwood," Mrs. Astor's place and "Beaulieu" which had belonged to Lord Astor before he sold it to the Vanderbilts, had something of the same dignified tradition which only age can give. And no doubt the real charm of Newport is still in these old homes and always will be.

But "Marble House," which cost ten million dollars to build, had to pay such heavy taxes that Mrs. Belmont's heirs could hardly look upon it as a summer "cottage" to cherish. They sold it. And a change of ownership in the "show places" makes it quite evident that the fame of Newport was not merely in its marble and bricks. Several years after Cornelius Vanderbilt, Sr., died everyone noticed that the "Breakers" and the big house on Fifth Avenue were never opened the same year; the widow's income could hardly have supported such tremendous expense. Though the income he left his widow was very generous indeed, living expenses were increasing so much—this accounts for it.

Southampton and other resorts had the advantage, too, of being near enough New York so that those who came out for the week-end could have a few hours of golf or tennis before dinner; it cost much less in time to get there.

Even in the height of its favor it was disconcerting for the Newport hostesses to see their ephemeral men-guests excuse themselves Sunday evening before dinner was over and dash down to catch the boat. They did not change from their evening clothes, their bags would be waiting for them in their cabins—and they could sleep as long as they liked next morning after the boat had docked in the early dawn. No one wanted to be placed at dinner between the "boat men"

Brown Brothers, photo.

TENNIS TOURNAMENT AT THE NEWPORT CASINO

or even have one on the right or left, for before the end of the meal there would be only a vacant chair to talk to. I heard one woman complaining to her host: "Why did you put me between two boat men?" She had taken it quite personally.

Some of the Newport summer colony had season tickets on these boats: there were two five-dollar cabins de luxe which were the climax of the Fall River Line's achievement in those days; they were usually retained for Sunday evening, the season through, by someone in the colony who knew they would be regular guests who would have to be at business in New York Monday morning.

But the changes at Newport were no greater than those which began just before the War to take place in New York. When Mrs. Astor died the alteration was noticeable. Even the society reporter had a way of appreciating Mrs. Astor which was never transferred to any of the other "leaders" who competed for supremacy afterwards.

"She is the most simple and unaffected of all the women of note in American society," one of the papers wrote. "In conversation she does not use the broad 'a' so much affected by most smart women in this country. Her manner is almost old-fashioned in its mingling of simplicity with stateliness. . . . She goes to church as faithfully as a woman of two generations ago, holding pews in four different churches."

And when she used to stand in one of them, holding the hymn-book with her son and singing, a fellow parishioner said that he was fascinated by her "head lights"—the two great solitaire diamonds she wore in her ears.

"She has an amount of personal dignity," the writer continues, "with all her graciousness, that flavors of noblesse oblige, and is said to have a great restraining influence on the more frivolously inclined in her own set than all other influences combined. . . . Mrs. Astor was the only woman living who had the power to maintain a semblance of real exclusiveness. . . . Her power has not been disputed."

And since her power was not disputed she did not have to resort to extravagance to maintain it; she was not rivalling other women but leading them. She had been born into old New York as a Schermerhorn—she had married an Astor. When her balls were the great social event of the winter, the favors at her cotillions were far from what they became later. One of them rejoiced in favors which were nothing more than very lovely paper butterflies, each one at the end of a wand. And what made that ball unique was that the ballroom itself seemed full of butterflies which lit upon the lovely gowns of the dancers, upon the black and white of the men's evening clothes, upon the walls and even upon those innumerable gilt chairs.

This profusion of natural beauty was scathingly commented upon in one newspaper as evidence of the supreme cruelty of the "Four Hundred," who were willing that thousands of fragile little creatures should be sacrificed for an evening of pleasure.

The very amiable fact was that the effect of butterflies in swift motion was given by a cinema camera concealed in the musicians' balcony at one end of the ballroom.

Today such ideas for enlivening a formal ball would seem, I suppose, quite childish. But today the cabaret, the dancing in any restaurant where the floor has been left clear, puts the ball itself in an antiquated category. Today the magnificence of the music-hall in its appeal to a public, growing more and more exigent, has pushed the personal entertainment into the background. But I doubt if social life has benefited from this change.

Cotillion favors would make a story in themselves: the discussion beforehand by the hostess and her advisor; the curiosity—and I grieve to say, greed—of the guests before they arrived; the criticism or astonished pleasure once they had been distributed: little gold axes for a Washington's Birthday cotillion, gold vanity boxes when such things were a novelty, jewelled belt pins, fans, Louis XV canes and the whole gamut of unessentials which could become spectacular, if enough were spent upon them.

I recall that on the famous occasion when Mrs. Pembroke-Jones had Sherry's whole floor done over in rose-pink velvet and brocade for one evening, there was a woman who suddenly grew exclusive and announced she was *not going*. But when she heard there were to be diamond bangles for the ladies and diamond stickpins for the men, she changed her mind!

Yet serene as Mrs. Astor's story reads, it used to be said that when she assumed the scepter to rule New York society it was then that Waldorf Astor went to England. And there, where his mansion had stood, rose up the first of the gigantic hotels which were to become a sign of the age and do more than we realize to take from the homes the aureole of elegance and prestige.

Among those who followed Mrs. Astor in point of time, if not in legendary glory, there was no one who cared to put too much emphasis on formality. Mrs. Belmont liked not to be too exclusive; Mrs. Fish liked above all to have her own way and not be restrained by any sort of rule; it might be that had someone established the tone which would have combined the past with the present—as in English society it is done instinctively—there might not have been what we must realize is a dissolving of what, for want of a better name, we call "Society"—with a capital "S."

The Leaders of Society were the high priests. Whoever they were, and whoever their followers were, they were *all* playing for power; a word which ought to be spelled with a capital too.

To have acknowledged power it was necessary to have wealth. Not to have wealth would have been to have only a straw crown in a madhouse. Diamond tiaras were not empty symbols. "The Queens" wore them; their followers wore them, of all sizes, shapes and values. We were classed by our jewels—and they differed in beauty and in value. . . .

"Look at her tiara!" said Mrs. Kernochan of the sibilant "S's." "Those are not diamonds, those are oyster-shells!"

And there was really never but one queen, for the tradition of Mrs. Astor does stand alone. Ward Mc-Allister and Harry Lehr were never more than prime ministers to Mrs. Astor. There were of course kings of industry, railroad kings, financial czars and emperors, and there were the "coal barons"—a title with feudal distance in it, but all these were too busy to consider society as a serious game even though every one of them wanted his wife to succeed at it no matter what it cost. It cost a great deal; not merely in money but in the effort to keep the position you had gained or were born into, against all newcomers; in the effort to go forward all the time towards the position held by the Leaders of Society. Success there meant incalculable triumph and power,—incalculable because it was so vague and because there were such indefinite limits to the use of power.

Lady Paget, who had been Minnie Stevens of Newport, used to ask: "Just what is it that you are all after anyway?"

No one could tell her, although she had a right to

the answer because she had been the belle of Newport —had never been rich, and when she married Arthur Paget, had married for love. It was only a long time afterwards that she became a "Lady."

In England, she said, all the effort was to get the Prince of Wales as a guest, to have him frequent your house. That was a goal which she understood; the terrific competition in American Society she found nothing but a confusion of mind and a fatigue of body.

There is more than a chapter which might be called "the Break-up" in the picture which Cornelius Vanderbilt, Jr., gives of the fine old house at 677 Fifth Avenue being now a shoe-shop, instead of the place where Andrew Carnegie used to try to impress the eight-year-old boy that it took genius to hang on to money, the place where Andrew Mellon regarded the sandwiches and cakes "with gazelle-like eyes," where the maternal grandfather regarded with disdain the noisy and exuberant Frick of Pittsburgh.

Richard T. Wilson, who was Cornelius' grandfather, was very proud of being a Georgian and looked down on the man of that town which—had not the British got it away from the French—would have been called Duquesne. The settlers of Georgia might well look any way they wished at a man from Fort Pitt, founded in 1759 and later to be called Pittsburgh.

The emphasis which Americans put upon ancestors may seem absurd to those who have never asked the names of their grandfathers, but it means more than wealth.

The châteaux and the fine old houses have changed so little in the last hundred years—except when they have been subjected to modern improvements—that it is easy to realize what a contrast there must be between what is within and what is without for those who have lived in them all their life. I recall that the Count Antoine de Nicolaÿ used to say that when he was a child in the house on the rue de Lille there was never any noise in the big courtyard in the morning such as his very robust and energetic concierge felt she had the perfect right to make with sweeping and shaking of her rugs or summoning her equally robust and energetic offspring.

Yet when I told him the story which I had heard that the nobles in their feudal castles used to keep the children of the villagers up all night to beat the ponds so that the frogs would not croak and disturb their august slumbers he could not believe that it was founded on fact. He had never heard of such tyranny, and history had been, he said, too often falsified to warrant his accepting the tale.

Whether true or false the present owners of old estates are much more likely today to be the victims of habit and custom—legal customs—than the persons whom they employ. I know one chatelain who wanted to dismiss the gardener, whose little house was the old lodge and just at the entrance of the grounds, because of the increasing number of illegitimate grandchildren every year more visible and audible. But the law would not allow him to dispossess the worthy ancestor on such grounds. He had to find him another situation to his (the gardener's) taste, it seemed. What to do? He knew that the gardener had a way of taking the best of the fruits and vegetables and so he laid in wait for him. Sure enough one morning, there he was picking the first fruits with the fine assurance of a connoisseur.

The chatelain sprang out at him and gave him a good drubbing and warned him of harsher measures should he catch him again alone. As he was not unable physically to keep his word, the gardener soon found another place—and moved.

Mrs. Belmont had a longer wait before she could be released—legally—from an inefficient watchman, to whom she gave the use of a quaint and adequate little cottage on her beautiful place at Beaulieu—called "Isoletta." The only drawback to this site on the Mediterranean was that the railroad tracks ran so close to the house that you had to cross them to get into the grounds.

"I'm going to make you a present," Tessie Oelrichs said to Mrs. Belmont one day when we had got over the ties and rails.

"Ah?" said Mrs. Belmont, hopefully.

"A new entrance," said Mrs. Oelrichs, "one that goes under those tracks."

Mrs. Belmont's face fell.

"I'd rather give you the place itself than have a tunnel."

"And I wouldn't take your house as it is, with a string of pearls about it."

It looked worthy of pearls though, for it was a coral pink with blue shutters in good "Midi" style. Nor was it merely the discomfort of crossing the tracks which bothered us—it was the fact that there was a curve one way and a tunnel the other beyond the grounds so that you could not see the train, coming in either direction, until it was almost on you. Added to that, it came from the left—as railroads do in France, following the English fashion, while your own cars and the tram just beyond the tracks took the right side. You had to be nimble sometimes.

The midnight express thundered by and shook the house as it rattled and tore its way south.

I never pretended to try to go to sleep until that train had passed and I was so obsessed with the idea that during its noisy passage anyone who wanted to could break a window or ten windows without being heard, that Mrs. Belmont finally sent to Paris for iron shutters.

As there was no house anywhere near—except that of her own farmer—she had engaged the watchman. To be sure that he would watch she always had him served strong black coffee when he came on duty and she provided him with the liveliest French "penny dreadfuls" that she could get. This gave us a certain peace of mind until one night, waking and putting on the light in the boudoir next her bedroom, Mrs. Belmont went to the glass-door and peered through the curtains.

There was the watchman comfortably stretched out on all the fur rugs which he had pulled to the floor for his greater ease. On the little table by him was his revolver.

Mrs. Belmont slipped on a dressing-gown, opened the door noiselessly, crossed the hall, stepped over the sleeping guardian and took the revolver; she put it in her room. Then she went back and poked the man with an umbrella until he woke up and listened to her lecture. But he assured her that nothing could have happened.

"Indeed!" she retorted. "Anyone could have come in here, taken your revolver from the table."

Quite naturally he looked at the table—his firearm was gone! He looked apprehensively at the hall-door. When she told him *she* had taken it he was not exactly relieved. Then she dismissed him.

At least she thought she had done so until she began to learn all the legal difficulties which lay between the wish and the deed in France. In the end, however, he too found another place as gardener without nocturnal responsibilities and left.

Even though she had a maid sleep in the room next, Mrs. Belmont never felt very safe in that lovely bedroom of hers next her boudoir but she would not give in to her fear, and pretended to believe that the French bulldog which slept in her maid's room was enough protection.

But one night during Mrs. Belmont's absence in New York that same maid, aroused by the barking of the dog, opened her door and switched on the light to see a man's head—a blond head of hair which she had never seen before—coming up from the floor below. She turned the light off, slammed her door and clambered out of her window on to the terrace on that side. She ran across the second terrace to the house of the farmer. She had seen another man waiting in the garden down below.

The farmer dashed out of his cottage and hailed a late automobilist who was passing and asked to be taken to the police station. The police heard the story, but said they had no car and could not come until morning. The obliging person with the car told them to pile in and he'd take them back.

And when the police arrived and the maid came limping back she found the man had entered by throwing a heavy stone through the iron shutters of one of the dining-room windows, under cover of the midnight express. The doors by which the burglar had left were wide open—but nothing was missing; they were frightened off too soor.. And my theory about windows and express trains was justified. It was by a broken window that the intruder had reached that staircase.

It was here—to this beautiful "Isoletta" at Beaulieu—
that Mrs. Belmont, full of sympathy for a hard-working
interior decorator and "antiquaire," invited her.

"I am going to give her a two weeks' vacation," she
told me, "which will not cost her a cent from the time
she leaves her room to the time she gets back!"

So she enquired the cost of a first-class ticket on the
train de luxe and added money for taxis, porters, and
dining car tips and sent off the check, covering it
all with the invitation to join her at her home on the
Mediterranean.

The woman arrived and confided to me with
much amusement that, as she had come down third-
class and carried her own lunch and her own suit-case,
she had saved a lot out of that check for use in the
doubtful future. I don't know whether or not she
boasted to her hostess of this far-sightedness.

Plans were made which included the usual drives,
opera and dinners at Monte Carlo. "But in the morning," said Mrs. Belmont with emphasis, "I work in
here [her study]. I am writing my memoirs and I must
be alone."

What was her surprise the very next morning to see
the door of her study open.

"Now I'm not going to disturb you," said her guest,
"I'll just sit over here and knit."

Work—unless she was quite alone—being impossible,
her hostess suggested a walk. That morning would
have to be counted as lost. The next morning, before

the guest could get into the room, the key was turned
in the lock. Finding she could not get in she went to
the garden just outside, where Mrs. Belmont could
hear her giving orders to the men who were working
there:

"Put the bench here and the vase over there," she
said, "and do not bring the bushes so far this way."

Down went the pen and bang went the door; the
guest's orders had to be countermanded at once if the
garden was to be as the owner of the house wanted it.
Another morning lost!

With commendable antiquarian zeal, the lady then
began to urge the purchase of some chairs she had seen
in town. But Mrs. Belmont having just ordered from
her house in America what she needed saw no reason
for buying others. She said so and thought she had
brought the argument to its fitting close.

But not so her guest: that afternoon after various
errands they were to meet in the main square of the
town and drive home together. When Mrs. Belmont
got there she found her guest seated in the middle of
a long row of chairs.

"I asked the dealer to put them out in a strong
light," she said, "so that you could get their full effect."

"Well, I've got it," said Mrs. Belmont, "and now he
can take them in again."

The visit was to have lasted two weeks but the ex-
asperation of the hostess had reached its climax at the
end of the first week.

"If that woman does not leave," she said, "I shall go mad!"

And that afternoon when the guest came into her room from a walk she had taken alone, she found a corner of the ceiling was soaking, water was dripping from it over the floor; buckets of water were standing about; the rug was up and the furniture was moved back. Her hostess was lamenting noisily.

"That leak again!" she said, her eyes fixed on the ceiling, "and the plumber not even in town—gone to San Raphael for a funeral and won't be back for three days! We can't do a thing until he comes back!"

The astonished guest, much worried, looked about for her belongings.

"Your things?" said Mrs. Belmont. "I have had them taken to the hotel where I engaged a room for you. I could not—I simply could not let you stay in this room."

And then, turning to the man who was frenziedly mopping and pushing things about:

"For goodness' sake, Jean, get another pail!"

And the lady-decorator never guessed, I am sure, that, for two hours during her absence, that man had been up on the ladder sopping the ceiling with a sponge, and that he had besides spilled water on the floor and brought in other buckets of it for scenic purposes.

MRS. OLIVER H. P. BELMONT'S FRENCH CHÂTEAU, SEINE ET MARNE

CHAPTER XXII

PAGEANTRY

THE LOVE OF JEWELS AND THE LOVE OF CLOTHES ARE very often the love of the pageant. Yet those who indulge in either must have the excuse of being—as are the Maharajahs—from countries where pageantry still exists or—as artists and actors are—a little to one side of the accepted monotony of life.

Men, ordinarily, have so little chance to be "different" that they have to content themselves with making a choice of details, but even the color of gloves, spats or cravats may mark them as being too original to be taken seriously. Yet vanity is theirs, for I remember that at a certain European water-cure, Mrs. Oelrichs wanted the same room for her boy's tutor that she had had the year before.

"Impossible, Madam," said the hotel clerk, "the Prince of X. has his tailor in it."

"His *tailor?*"

"Yes, Madam, to take in his clothes during the 'cure'—as he gets thinner."

She did not press the matter. The Prince being one of the fattest men at the Cure, she watched with interest for him to diminish. He did—and his clothes, she told me, fitted perfectly at every stage.

An Italian countess I once knew, who was neither artist nor actress—professionally—had her whole life changed, I believe, by being told that she resembled Sarah Bernhardt. From that day she had something to live for and, having married a very rich man, she could live for it: dress as she supposed Bernhardt might were all the world—or at least Rome and Venice—a stage.

The first time I saw her she was wearing an all-gold costume, not unlike that of Bernhardt's in "Gismonda"; she always had vermilion lips—this, long before they were considered possible in a drawing-room —and, at times, turquoise blue hair; she affected enormously long gloves of black or white or gold and ample Florentine sleeves of black velvet embroidered in gold.

But she did not limit her love of the exotic to her clothes; she had richly plumaged parrots and monkeys which, not having any plumes of color, she dressed in Louis XV costumes, feathered hats and all. You were likely to find one hanging upside down from a branch in the garden with the hoop-skirts falling over its head or the panache hat rakishly set above an ugly little visage, too unpleasantly resembling a human. Her prize pet however was a boa-constrictor upon whose length of writhing evil she had put turquoise bracelets —on elastic bands.

How this lady's sensibilities had been so super-re-
fined when she had risen to her position from an extremely modest one—her father was a wall-paper manu-
facturer—it is hard to explain, unless you take into account the influence of her reputed likeness to the great
Sarah.

But that refinement took strange twists as, for instance, when she could not bear the jarring notes of
her guests' clothes in what she considered a perfectly
appointed room, harmonizing with her own gowns. To
avoid the discomfort of this possible dissonance she
hung black velvet curtains with slits for the limited
number of heads of those who were at her receptions.

In this subtle fashion they could communicate but
leave her own color scheme unjostled and serene.
Whether anyone so tyrannically used ever came again
I could not say. Her love of black velvet in the home
seemed almost to exclude color, for when Boldini, by
appointment and dreaming of an exceptional subject
for a portrait, saw her for the first time in her own
house he found the effect funereal, sepulchral. As he
entered the dimly lighted room where she was awaiting him, he saw that the center of the floor was paved
—as it were with mirrors; upon that flooring were
black velvet pillows in profusion, and stretched upon
the pillows in the costume of Eve was the Countess,
pale as a corpse.

Boldini left precipitately and whenever he referred
to what was to him a gruesome spectacle he used to

cover his eyes with his two hands and groan: "Mère LaChaise! Mère LaChaise!"

He painted some wonderful portraits of her—one with a Russian wolfhound, large black hat and bunch of violets.

When we were in Venice and had a well-known and extremely distinguished-looking man in our gondola on the Grand Canal one afternoon, we met the Countess in hers; she was magnificently dressed, in tribute to Venetian splendor, I presume, and had one of her monkeys in conscious or unconscious caricature of that splendor, and one of her parrots—the boa-constrictor was evidently left in Paris.

On reaching home our guest found an invitation to dine with the lady who was a complete stranger the same evening. Having heard of her eccentricities he was not surprised in the garden of her palazzo, where he had been taken, to be greeted by her in an amazing costume of gold-colored turkish trousers and velvet jacket—and this was before the days of informal pyjamas. He bowed over her hand in as ceremonial a manner as he could summon and followed her silent guidance in to dinner. She spoke not a word.

They were served an exquisite meal by servants who seemed peculiarly "stylized" and hushed. He waited for her to open the conversation, determined not to let himself in for some breach of her chosen etiquette. She ate in silence and so did he, observing her with gallant politeness, a response hovering upon his lips should it

Fiorillo, Paris, photo.

THE AUTHOR IN COURT COSTUME
Presentation at Buckingham Palace, 1931
From the Portrait by Mrs. Leslie Cotton

be called for.

But not a word did she utter during the long meal!

Nor was any other word spoken as they went into the gloaming of the garden to be served their coffee. So he too was mute. Finally he rose, bent again over her hand, and summoned his gondolier by a gesture. From her point of view it must have been just what she had wanted, for she gave him a ravishing smile as he left.

All this excessive languor of manner was perhaps but a symptom of madness, for quite often her butler would say to callers—this was in Paris after she had been, for her very extravagances, divorced by the Count—that "Madame is absent—she is in the Maison de Santé," as they politely call insane asylums in France.

The madness may, however, have been assumed, for it was noticed that she went into retreat about the time that bills were being somewhat vociferously presented. One of the saleswomen of a couturière I knew was astonished to hear this same devoted Italian butler suggest, during the absence of the Countess, that she go up to the wardrobe and take back that which had not been paid for—"or whatever you think would compensate you," he added.

One time, when she was staying at the Danielli, she announced to a caller that she had been so extravagant in buying her latest pets that she had not been able to pay her maid for two months.

"Let me show them to you," she said, leaning over one of the several baskets which he had noticed without much curiosity when he had come into the little salon.

She opened it and lifted out a serpent. . . . "One of the rarest kind in the world," she said intensely.

As she put it back and started to open a larger and more imposing basket, the gentleman left without saying good-bye.

"If I had known," he said, "that I was sitting there waiting for her, surrounded by reptiles . . ."

One of them did get away later at the Ritz in Paris and there was great excitement in the hotel until it was found—by the valet of Sir Francis Bertie, the British ambassador, who was staying there temporarily while the Embassy was having repairs done. The snake had got into the bed—but fortunately while it was empty!

The last time I saw her I saw nothing but her—quite literally. We were a group lunching with friends who lived in the apartment above the one occupied by the Countess. This was on the ground floor and led into the garden.

"Isn't the garden lovely?" asked our hostess, pulling aside the curtains to show it to us . . . then she gasped and so did we, for there upon the shaded path, the palms of her hands held up towards the sky, was the Countess in complete undress—not a stitch on her. She seemed oblivious to the world and was, apparently, talking to herself.

The curtain was quickly drawn and we retired from viewing the garden. Some inquiry on the part of our hostess later brought the information that her Mahatma had told the Countess how to regain the love of the man who had just deserted her: she must walk unadorned in broad daylight with an offering in her hands and an invocation upon her lips. She had followed the advice.

But whether she was successful . . .

The influence of Venice has always been very great; it made extravagance itself into a ritual, as for instance, in that custom in medieval times of the Pisani family throwing all the gold dishes used at a banquet into the Canal, so that they should apparently never serve again—a more costly form of breaking the glass in which has been drunk a toast.

Even in those days, they did have that net fastened under water and drew it up with its contents as soon as the honored guests had gone.

Napoleon knew no fiercer way of showing his power at Venice than by destroying all the Doges' regalia and robes, burning them and the "Bucentaure." And there could be no more significant way of ushering in a new era—but I have never forgiven him. Pageantry ought not to be destroyed!

CHAPTER XXIII

THE CORONATION OF GEORGE VI

AND PAGEANTRY IS NOT DEAD!

There before me was an Indian Prince in his costume of heavy white satin shot with gold, a turban whose front—even though I could not see it—I knew was richly jewelled, and the black boots which make such striking contrast to the rich fabrics and enhance them. . . .

And before him lords and ladies, their crimson robes over their arms and their coronets in their hands. . . .

We were walking down what, in the directions given to each one of us, was called "the covered way," to the entrance which had been designated under "No. 1," for those who had a big "2" in the upper corners of their card of convocation to the Coronation of George VI and his Queen.

It was only half-past seven o'clock in the morning, but the doors of Westminster Abbey had been open since six.

There had been no Indian Prince in that book of Chivalry which my father had given me when I was ten years old and which had had such an overpowering influence on me that I had learned all about heraldry before I was grown and had never been tired of those combinations of colors and symbols which made up the coats of arms of the knights in that old book—and in many others.

The entrance engulfed this image of Indian magnificence and he became part of the medieval setting, in which we found ourselves as we crossed the threshold of the Annex, built for this occasion. Once inside, it seemed to me that it must always have been there, a generous vestibule to the austere Abbey with its hundreds of famous tombs—today, as the programs put it quite frankly—a theatre.

The old-gold color of the walls of the Annex—or as someone described it, "fawn-color"—was a background for the tapestries from Buckingham Palace; the Axminster carpet was of royal blue—this was what I saw after we had come in from the Broad Sanctuary, as that space north of the Abbey is so oddly called.

"Broad Sanctuary" and "covered way"; and my car had been told to keep to "the crown of the road"—the very wording of the directions added to my sense of having stepped into another world. We had been told as peers and peeresses "to assume the robes" of our "Estate"; and "shown" was written "shewn."

But we were not allowed to pause in the Annex; a man in gorgeous medieval costume, a Gold Staff Officer, was spreading out the train of my robe, and I passed through into the Abbey itself; *I was part of the pageant!*

In that famous Blue Parlor at Saratoga, when I was a child, you may remember I mentioned that I had walked down a blue carpet towards the mirror at the end of that long, long room, and felt so small in its immensity, extending on as it did into the mirror. And here, after so many years of eager watching for even the tatters of pageantry which modern life still offers now and then, in some masquerade or formal ceremony, in some ball or at the opera, I was lost in another immensity, walking upon a blue carpet which covered historic stones, which ran between two tiers of balconies where I could see—although it was so early in the day—hundreds of court costumes, with waving feathers, and hundreds of brilliant uniforms.

To be part of this earliest procession! One of the hundreds who would be passing up the long stretch of royal blue carpet, preceded by others who were going to sit at the left or the right when they reached the great transept. There had been nothing in that book of mine to suggest this. Yeomen of the guard on either side who had come from the Tower of London—the Tower of London!

Pageantry was not dead! History was coming alive before my eyes!

We walked very slowly; no one stepped on the train of the one in front—and the color!—the red velvet and the ermine or miniver with that remnant of what had been a velvet hood centuries ago, hanging between the ermine-covered shoulders of the peers—Gold Staff Offi-

ELIZABETH, LADY DECIES IN THE ROBES SHE WORE AT THE
CORONATION OF GEORGE VI

cers with their truncheons—shorter than in the days of
Louis XIV when they were staffs of dignity and not for
use; these were to be used to point with, red in the
middle and gilded at either end. A Gold Staff Officer
was showing me where I was to sit in the North Transept—I had kept my eyes straight ahead of me and so
I had seen it all as you see a dream at the moment of
waking.

There were nine chairs on either side of the aisle,
and after the sixth row each row was a step higher up.
Ample chairs upholstered in the same royal blue and
with gold galons and the King's monogram and crown
embroidered in red and gold in the upper right hand
corner of the back. My name on a card showed me my
chair. Nothing had been left to chance.

The peers were across from us in that part of the
transept called "the Poets' Corner." Ladies could
search out their lords and imagine them conversing si-
lently with ancient bards, but the distance would be
too great to hear what was being said, for from the
back row of the peeresses' seats to the back row of peers
it was more than two hundred feet.

When I arrived, the chair on either side of me was
already occupied.

We talked. Everyone was talking. It seemed more
than odd, it even shocked me for a moment that no one
seemed to be thinking of Westminster Abbey as a
church; nor did the mood seem to change even when
the light high voices of the choir boys rang out in the

anthem. Yet although not churchly it was serious—out there where they kept on coming along the blue carpet in their gorgeous clothes. The four Knights of the Garter wearing that rich blue velvet robe which is their right, with the white satin breeches, white stockings—and the garter—and white shoes with rosettes! They would be holding a cloth-of-gold canopy over the King while he was being anointed.

Queen Mary's box was empty except for the Earl and Countess of Strathmore, Queen Elizabeth's parents. And all the way up to the roof there was color of uniform and white feathers, tier above tier of balconies. . . .

"Oh, dear!" exclaimed one of my neighbors, "I knew it would happen!"

She had let her coronet slip from her lap and it had fallen under the chair in front. There was no room for her to lean over and reach for it.

"My coronet is under your chair," she said to the peeress in front of her, who amiably retrieved it and handed it back.

Some of the peeresses had put ribbons to their coronets and held them on their arms like handbags, for there was so much to hold—the program of the ceremony, in foolscap size, bound in blue paper, the prayer book in white with the royal coat-of-arms in gold, and the bag in which you carried cough-drops and smelling-salts and a lorgnette and luncheon tickets for the House of Lords. We could not put on our coronets until the Queen was crowned. When we saw the Queen being anointed we put everything but the coronet on our chairs—and when we put the coronet on, we did it all together, holding it in our two hands, placing it upon our heads carefully and sticking the two little coronet-pins through our hair. It must have made quite a picture, for the peers who had been wearing their coronets ever since the King was crowned. They could see all the white-gloved arms lifted at once, holding the head-dress, wavering over it for a moment and then descending.

An artist with prophetic vision had painted the scene for one of the magazines and with great diplomacy he made all the peeresses not only young and beautiful but slender; it must have been looking at this illustration in color which gavé the poetic words to a newspaper reporter who wrote: that "the peeresses all 'lifted' their coronets to their heads with the lovely sweeping motion of a host of swans' necks arching towards the dawn of a new day."

But the peers' coronets were heavier than ours, which had been made small in order to fit in behind tiaras. . . .

"Don't they look like choir-boys, bare-headed and in their white capes?" said my other neighbor.

To my sight they all looked much happier when they finally had their hands freed from holding the symbols of their "estate." In the old days I suppose they did have hatracks for helmets. There were hatracks at the

House of Lords, where we had lunch after the Coronation. I saw coronets piled upon them in strange democratic fashion. More than that, when one of the earls put his on to leave, I saw a bright bit of orange decoration which certainly had not been there during the ceremony. I could not see what it was. A second and a third coronet, decorated in the same way, had passed me before I recognized a hat-check which had not been unpinned from the velvet headpiece!

"I wish I had brought my opera glasses," said Lady Glanusk. "Then I could see what the Queen is wearing on her head."

I told her that without opera glasses I could see that the Queen had nothing upon her head. But that did not please her.

"She may be wearing a string of beads that you can't see," she insisted. "The liturgy says that women must have their heads covered."

I did not say that I thought that if she had, it would make putting on the crown quite a complicated ceremony. I saw the Queen's dark hair, with its unswerving part, quite unadorned until she had her lovely crown set upon it.

"The liturgy says 'a crown of pure gold,'" said Lady Glanusk when that great moment had arrived, "and it isn't gold at all; it is platinum set with diamonds."

"Perhaps the 'gold' is symbolical," I said, for to me all that I was seeing had speech in it, heraldic speech, chivalrously spoken!

But it was odd—for the liturgy unfolds that to me—that the men who, it was said, must be there with heads bare were wearing caps of red velvet trimmed most meaningly with ermine or miniver and surmounted by their coronets and the women who were supposed by the liturgy to be covering their heads wore nothing but tiaras. How interpret such contradictions?

Yet it must be just as it was intended to be for had we not been rehearsed two days before to learn what must be worn, and what must be done at each stage of the ceremony. More than that here were printed directions which, under the genius of the Duke of Norfolk as Earl Marshal, had been clearly expressed in no uncertain terms. Nothing had been left to personal impulse or to the imagination. It was written that the chauffeur must have his lunch with him and not desert his car wherever he was officially parked. There must be a card with a large "L" on it on our windshield if we intended to lunch at the House of Lords. We must get out of our cars "with dispatch" at the "setting down" and no footman or chauffeur was to get off his seat—the Gold Staff Officer would help us out. And if we did not appear at once when, after the ceremony, our cars were announced the car would go off and leave us—and no one could promise that it would get back again!

Yet it was just these explicit directions which were making everything go so smoothly, and so I knew that some time or other the head-coverings and the lack of them would be explained. At any rate nothing had been done at the rehearsals which was not essential— even though to the detached observer the idea of rehearsals might seem to rob the approaching ritual of its spontaneous quality.

History had discreetly noted some of the embarrassments of ancient coronations which had been unrehearsed, embarrassments which might take from the solemnity of the hour. Even certain changes had been made several coronations back, as for example, when the noble, who was supposed to ride into the Abbey on horseback and fling down the glove so that anyone who wished might challenge the right of the king to his throne, had not been able to make his horse behave and had ridden in backward in spite of himself—a ceremonial not at all to the taste of the peers or their sovereign! Thereafter that part of the ceremony was omitted.

And when Queen Victoria, during her coronation, had been given the golden orb and had asked naïvely: "What shall I do with this?"

"Hold it, and it please Your Majesty," the Archbishop of Canterbury had replied.

Greater changes, too, had taken place which were making this coronation like none that had preceded it —changes which to Edward the Confessor would have seemed purest magic—dangerous magic perhaps. We were hearing distinctly—as everyone else—all that was being said there on the stage of the "theatre." We could look across to where they were speaking, but their voices were *above us*—just where, we could not tell: the magic of an amplifier.

And we knew, too, although there was no visible evidence of it, that other magic was taking place: this whole scene was being photographed for the cinema.

Quite close to us in the North Transept there was a tomb—the tomb of Aymer de Valence, ancient enemy of Robert Bruce—and above his recumbent figure a box had been built for the camera operators and a slit in the wall through which the cameras were focussed upon the thrones and the Royal box above them.

The photographers were catching everything but the color of the blue and gold brocades which hung from all those tiers of balconies that had been built for this one occasion—over all the balconies but two, those which made the Royal box and the one above it filled with royal guests from other countries; these were hung with plain cloth of gold which served as background for the magnificent Westminster plate, standing there on a sort of buffet behind the King and Queen.

Below all this gold, the gold-colored carpet upon which the thrones on their platforms and the faldstool were placed. And leading up to the theater, that straight line of rich blue carpet, whose weaving they said had cost more than sixty thousand pounds—a blue width unbroken except where a piece had been cut out of it for the tomb of the Unknown Soldier buried under its wreath of blood-red roses which the King and Queen had sent.

All this color in the framework of dark stone walls and clustered columns which had been there so many centuries that they show their age, as they rose up in Gothic strength, in the shadows upon them. But even that encircling grey was broken by the stained glass windows through which a brighter and brighter day was coming in until—just as the King was being anointed his head was touched by a ray of sunlight, carrying with it all the rainbow colors of medieval glass.

What a splendid promise!

Before the ceremony of the crowning had taken place we had sat there watching the processions of the Princes of the Church, Their Majesties, Queen Mary, that Royal figure, the Queen of Norway and all the other Royalties and High Dignitaries in this "minster" built by the first Edward just before William the Norman arrived. *He* had been crowned here! And before that crowning it had been his colored tents, the variegated costumes of his followers, the banners and plate which had dazzled the eyes of the Saxons and aroused their covetousness. . . . Pageantry had come in with the Norman—but Westminster Abbey in its austerity was already here! What we were seeing would never have been possible if either had been lacking.

On both tiers, all those who were seated here belonged either to the pageantry or to the austerity—in costume at least.

Outside were the millions who had seen all this in hours of approach, for London is so big and the ways leading to Westminster so many. I could only see it as it seated itself higher and higher in the Abbey, or came down that blue carpet towards the Crowning Ceremony—for once both figurative and literal!

Those Indian Princes whose suavity of color seemed to have the sound of mysterious words uttered softly! There was the Maharajah of Nepal wearing that casque of pearls which covered his head and ears, fringed with emeralds, decorated with a huge pearl-set emerald above his forehead, from which rose those long bird-of-paradise feathers—four times longer than any others in the world. At the opening of Parliament in November he had worn it to the amazement and admiration of all the women in the House of Lords. He had turned his head abruptly at the audible exclamations of several of them; the feathers had brushed my cheek. He apologized.

"I feel most conspicuous," he had said in perfect Oxford English!

Today, among the other Indian Princes, his casque was as always a matter of marvel, yet he was no longer so conspicuous but part of imperial color.

The peers would be in the picture. But there would be no photograph of the peeresses. We were not in the line of vision!

Yet what a design it would have made, all the robes being the same; those tassels which showed would be perhaps an irregular part of the design, for not all of us wore them in front—as the Queen was doing. Our faces would have appeared as faintly colored splotches of light, and the tiaras—of every size and shape, but all very brilliant—would have melted into the design, since you cannot photograph jewels *en masse* and the peeresses were ablaze with diamonds.

"What a spectacle!" said Lord Vivien to a group of us afterwards when we were taking lunch in the sacred precincts of the House of Lords. But *we* were not to see it! I felt like that woman whose husband having made his money unexpectedly asked his wife what she wanted. She wanted a beautiful house and she wanted diamonds and she wanted the finest make of automobile. And when she had them all, he said:

"Now you have everything you want, haven't you?"

"Oh, no, I haven't," she sighed.

"Well, what more do you want?"

"I want to sit on a fence," she said, "and see myself go by."

The King's sister, the Princess Royal, came in with the two little princesses, in their miniature robes; we expected to see them go up that slender staircase which led to the Royal box but instead she took the chair which the Duke of Gloucester was to occupy and two stools were produced for the small princesses: they were waiting for Queen Mary to take her place before they should take theirs.

In came the Duchess of Kent and the Duchess of Gloucester who bowed to the group as their long trains were put over their arms by their attendants, and they went up to their places. Then in came the Queen of Norway, the King's aunt—she stopped and spoke to the Princess Royal before she mounted.

At last, Queen Mary! She came down the blue carpet wearing that glistening silver and white gown and that rich blue ribbon of the Order of the Garter with its badge—her diamonds, her crown above white hair and all this dominated by her personality, enhanced by her own bearing! She bowed and spoke to her daughter and, after she had gone up to her place, they followed. Then we could see the two little heads bobbing above the cloth of gold or lifted towards Queen Mary whenever she spoke to them—as she did, from time to time, until the crowning of the King and of the Queen held her attention.

As the King left the first throne and went to that of St. Edward, he looked towards his mother. She bent her knee—that was to her King—she waved her hand, that was to her son. Then followed the enthronement and the homages.

Silver trumpets and the loud cry from all of us who belonged to the Empire—of "God Save the King."

Pageantry was living there before me!

INDEX

CPSIA information can be obtained
at www.ICGtesting.com
Printed in the USA
BVHW031718160819
556084BV00001B/9/P